The BIG BOOK *of* Relaxation

The BIG BOOK of Relaxation

EDITED BY LARRY BLUMENFELD

Simple Techniques to Control the Excess Stress in Your Life

THE RELAXATION COMPANY

Credits

Text

p. 10   From *The Wellness Book*, Herbert Benson, M.D. and Eileen M. Stuart, R.N., M.S. © 1992 the Mind/Body Medical Institute. Used by arrangement with Carol Publishing Group. A Birch Lane Press book.

p. 18   Excerpted from Bill Moyers's *Healing and the Mind* (Doubleday, 1993) © 1993 by Bill Moyers

p. 24   From "Meditation, the New Balm for Corporate Stress" by Geoffrey Smith, *Business Week* magazine. Reprinted by permission

p. 27   From "Om is Wher the Heart is" by Mary Talbot with John Schwartz, *Newsweek* magazine, February 5, 1992. Reprinted by permission.

p. 28   From *Hatha Yoga or The Philosophy of Physical Well-Being* by Yogi Ramacharaka, © 1930 Yogi Publication Society

p. 38   From "Yoga videos, a Good Way to Stretch your Fitness Regimen" by Nancy Hellmich, in *USA Today*. Reprinted by permission.

p. 50   From "Out to Lunch: Wolfing it Down, Living it Up and Every Course in Between", in *Cosmopolitan* magazine. Reprinted by permission.

p. 51   From "Fast Food, Slow Down!", by Jeanne Gordon in *Newsweek* magazine. Reprinted by permission.

p. 58   From a news story in *The New York Times*. Reprinted by permission.

p. 90   From *The Roar of Silence*, by Don G. Campbell © 1989 Quest Books.

p. 172   From *The Popcorn Report* by Faith Popcorn. © 1993 HarperCollins Publishers. All rights reserved.

The Creative Visualization chapter adapted from *Creative Visualization* by Shakti Gawain with permission from New World Library.

Art and Photography

p. 12: Three illustrations by Jeeni Criscenzo
Yoga: all photos by Dane Heithaus (including author photo)
Food: p. 55, 56, 57 — all photos by Jerry Orabona
Breath & Voice: p. 58 — David Lewiston
Aromatherapy: author photo by Kim Jew,
          p. 67, 69, 72, 73 — all photos by Jerry Orabona
Music: p. 95 — Harvey Lloyd/The Stock Market
Creative Visualization: author photo by Irene Young
Ohashiatsu: all photos by Larry Bercow (except author photo)
Conscious Exercise: p. 151 — Jerry Orabona

The publishers gratefully acknowledge the support and assistance of Lorryn Burns, Karen DiGesu, Carol Flax, Robert Folan, Jean Fredricks, Denise Goodson, David Greenfield, Kathryn Hall, Bonnie Harrington, Rob Johnson, Sandra Knell, Marcel Lavabre, Lana Michalko-Wraith, Joseph Mills, Rickie Navarro, Lora O'Connor, Susan Reich and the staff at Publishers Group West, Avis Rich, the staff at Tools for Exploration and Julianne Zaleta.

Editor: LARRY BLUMENFELD
Cover Design: BONNIE BUTLER
Interior Design: BARBARA GOLD / LOGO STUDIOS

Printed on recycled paper.

THE RELAXATION COMPANY

20 Lumber Road
Roslyn, NY 11576

CONTENTS

Preface

Life in the food chain can be a challenge. The elements rage; hunger dominates; the invading hordes are over the hill. And for human beings still facing these challenges—and many of us are—I regret that this book won't do much good.

For those of us who are adequately fed and clothed and basically free of imminent physical danger, however, the peculiar nature of life between the ears has created the need for a book like this.

Antelope don't get migraines. No insomnia amongst the frogs. Earthworms don't worry. It is that three pounds of cerebral cortex, our great big brain, which is the cause of our uniquely human stress and woe.

And our predicament is staggering. The physical pain, psychological distress, impaired functioning, physiological deterioration, sleep deprivation, digestive disorders, and on and on, which we endlessly endure are almost too overwhelming to face. The billions of pills popped, drinks drunk, and battles fought in our personal wars against stress are a testament to its powerful and immediate presence in our lives.

So stop it.

It was our intention in putting this book together to give you a concise, step-by-step guide to techniques that can make you feel much better and give you the control to stop the excess stress in your life. We sought out the most prominent and expressive authors in their respective fields and instructed them to be PRACTICAL... to tell you exactly what you need to do. We told the authors it was fine to include some background information, and we said it was all right to be inspiring, but without fail each chapter had to leave the reader with a clear idea of exactly what you could do today to begin mastering stress in your life.

Yet this book is useless.

We are very clear that, unless you actually give the techniques a try, this book is no more useful than a cookbook in the hands of someone who never cooks. Reading this book without trying out the practices and techniques will not have any value for you whatsoever. You will not be smarter, better-looking or richer and you certainly won't be any more relaxed.

The effort to relax is a sublime effort.

So few of us actually make the effort to relax as much as we think we should. Yet, relaxing isn't hard. Not in the way that running and weightlifting are hard. And, the results of relaxation are immediate and rewarding. It's not like flossing your teeth. There's no need to proceed on faith or theory like taking vitamins or only drinking filtered water. There's no addiction to overcome. You don't have to give up anything. It isn't expensive. It doesn't take a lot of time. What a strange fact that we don't all make the little efforts of relaxation on a consistent basis.

Part of the problem is that we take it for granted that we know how to relax, yet this isn't necessarily so. The techniques in this book should be part of every high school curriculum yet they remain outside of the general public dialogue. The four "r's" - reading, writing, 'rithmetic and relaxing should be part of basic education. The techniques work. They can free you up in marvelous ways. The choice is clear. Do you want to bear the slings and arrows of outrageous stress or take a few minutes and relax?

Jeffrey Charno
CEO & Founder
The Relaxation Company

CHAPTER 1

Meditation

John Harvey, Ph.D

Dr. John Harvey has been a student and teacher of meditation and yoga for over twenty years. In addition to other scientific publications, he has written a number of articles on the therapeutic and practical implications of meditation. He is editor of *The Quiet Mind: Techniques for Transforming Stress* (Himalayan Press).

Dr. Harvey is currently director of psychological services at Allied Services Rehabilitation Hospital in Scranton, Pennsylvania. He obtained his doctorate in Behavioral Disabilities at the University of Wisconsin-Madison, and served as an assistant professor of medical psychology at the University of Nebraska Medical Center before assuming his current position.

Current focuses of Dr. Harvey's clinical interests involve working with children, adolescents and adults with learning disabilities and attention-deficit disorder. He also directs programs for managing chronic pain as well as evaluating and serving individuals suffering from Alzheimer's Disease. He utilizes meditative techniques in his clinical practice.

*M*editation is the finest method available for creating relaxation at the mental level. It is the mental level where stress and tension are experienced in the most personal and persistent manner. Let us briefly consider the nature of mental stress before we define meditation and learn how to practice this simple yet highly effective tool for stress relief.

THE STRESS CYCLE

Perhaps the moment when most of us get the purest experience of mental stress is when we lie down and attempt to go to sleep. It is at this time that we face all of the impressions of the day that linger in varying degrees of intensity on the canvas of the mind. It is at this moment that we worry about all the tasks of the day which were not completed and we fret about the tasks that await us tomorrow. Our reactions and feelings toward others echo through our minds. And perhaps most importantly, we must face our evaluations and judgments about ourself. Small wonder that millions of people struggle to fall asleep, sleep poorly, and awaken the next morning with a tired body and a restless mind.

The next day begins and more impressions flood in followed by more reactions and concerns. The web of mental tension continually acquires more strands and with each day these strands become thicker. We feel more and more distracted. There are just too many things on our minds. It gets harder and harder to concentrate and we are more likely to make the kinds of errors, misperceptions, and poor decisions that lead to even greater worries. We feel increasingly exhausted, yet wound up, as the mental stress is immediately translated into physical tension and nervous energy. The cycle then feeds itself as tight muscles and a wired nervous system send signals to the brain that act to further increase mental tension. The cycle of mental to muscular tension is very persistent. Consequently, there can be no real experience of relaxation of the body until we learn to relax the mind.

Strictly speaking, the problem is not that the mind is so active, but rather the frenzied quality of this activity. In the tradition of yoga, the mind is referred to as the inner instrument. It is a faculty that can be used to perceive, to reason, to think creatively and intuitively, and to understand the self and the world. But like any instrument, it can be overused and

There can be no real experience of relaxation of the body until we learn to relax the mind.

misused, as in the scenario described above. Like any high-performance instrument, the mind needs proper care and maintenance. Meditation is really a method for taking care of this inner instrument and for transforming the quality of our mental activity.

WHAT MEDITATION IS AND ISN'T

Most of us have some misconceptions about meditation. We often connect it with the common dictionary definition, "to think deeply about or ponder." But meditation is a method of working with the mind, not a type of thinking. Meditation is a conscious effort to focus the mind in a non-analytic manner and to avoid discursive or ruminative thought.

Another common image is that meditation is linked to mysticism, occult religious practices and an acetic, withdrawn lifestyle. This is also an incorrect characterization. Meditation is really a practical technique to care for the mind that is most effectively practiced by people who are richly involved with life and who want to experience optimal health and well-being.

Along these lines, the scientific research on the benefits of meditation is quite compelling. People who regularly practice meditation show a dramatic decrease in stress symptoms. They show decreases in blood pressure, heart rate, levels of stress hormones and respiration rate. Regular meditators also seem to display a more adaptive response to stressful events in that they respond more dynamically yet recover more quickly.

Research studies have also shown that meditation has a positive influence on psychological well-being leading to increased self esteem, higher levels of self actualization and decreased anxiety and depression. In a therapeutic context, meditation has been successfully utilized to treat post-traumatic stress disorder, drug and alcohol addiction and chronic pain. And it seems that meditators as a group are in better overall health and require fewer health care services.

The term meditation is actually an English approximation for the Sanskrit word *dhyana*, which means an unbroken flow toward an object of meditation which might be an image, a word, a concept or the breath. Technically speaking, medita-

Meditation is really a practical technique to care for the mind that is most effectively practiced by people who are richly involved with life and who want to experience optimal health and well-being.

Discovering the Relaxation Response

In the late 1960s, my colleagues and I were conducting research on the causes and effects of hypertension. We were using biofeedback techniques to train squirrel monkeys—with a system of rewards and punishments—to control their blood pressure.

One day, several practitioners of transcendental meditation came to my office and told me they believed they could lower their blood pressure through the practice of meditation. They invited me to conduct research on them to validate this claim. It was 1968, and it was the Harvard Medical School; I was having difficulties even trying to convince my colleagues that stress might be related to hypertension. Not wanting to get involved with anything out of the mainstream, I politely showed them the door.

Persistent in their claims, the practitioners returned repeatedly until I agreed to measure key physiological responses. At the same time, at the University of California-Irvine, Drs. Robert Keith Wallace and Archie F. Wilson were conducting similar studies. We all found that several major physiological systems responded to the simple act of sitting quietly and giving the mind a focus: the metabolism decreased, the heart rate slowed, respiratory rate decreased, and there were distinctive brain waves. Maybe, I thought, these people had a point. Later, Dr. Wallace joined me at Harvard, and we continued our work together.

The evidence we gathered had compelling implications about the control you can exert over physiological functions. It suggested strongly that you could use your mind to change your physiology in a beneficial way, improve health, and perhaps reduce your need for medications. I subsequently coined the term "relaxation response" to describe this natural restorative phenomenon that is common to all of us.

—An anecdote from Dr. Herbert Benson, author of the best-selling *The Relaxation Response*, taken from *The Wellness Book* (Brich Lane/Carol Publishers)

tion is the second of three steps in a complete process. The first is concentration where the mind is focused on one thing rather than jumping from one distraction and worry to the next. As concentration is deepened the unbroken flow of meditation is achieved and one experiences freedom from distractions and disturbances and a profound sense of serenity.

The third step in the meditative process is called *samadhi* and refers to total absorption in the object of meditation. This is a state beyond normal thinking processes where an even deeper level of joy and peace is experienced and one obtains a penetrating insight into one's true nature. In summary, then, the process of meditation involves concentrating the mind, establishing an unbroken and continuous flow, and achieving absorption.

This all sounds fairly simple but, in fact, a certain degree of knowledge and skill is needed in order to successfully carry out and persist with the beneficial practice of meditation. The rest of this chapter will be devoted to step-by-step instruction in the actual practice of meditation.

Choosing a Time and Place

The first step is to choose a regular time and place for meditation that can be maintained day in and day out. Choose a time when other responsibilities will not interfere with your meditation and you won't create disturbances for the people you live with. Generally, early in the morning, late in the afternoon after work and at night before bed are suitable times for meditation.

Many people find that by getting up a few minutes early they can reliably set aside some time in the morning to meditate. This is a good time to meditate because the mind has not yet been flooded with impressions and the environment is likely to be quiet. Others find the afternoon or evening more convenient. Whatever time or times you choose, try to stick with them so that you are not faced with trying to make a decision each day as to when you will meditate. By adhering to a regular schedule, you will form a positive habit and your mind and body will spontaneously prepare for meditation.

In the same vein, it is helpful to have a regular place set aside for meditation. Ideally, select a place that is pleasant and quiet, has adequate fresh air and that typically isn't used for other purposes. Either a clean corner of a room or a spare room would be a fine location. As time goes on you will build an association with this spot and it will feel quite natural to sit there for your meditation.

Preparation

Just as it is with many important activities in life, preparation for meditation is important. The following guidelines for preparation shouldn't be seen as rigid rules, but as steps that can improve the quality of meditation.

Physical cleanliness helps to prepare you for meditation. Taking a shower or washing your face and hands before meditating will help you feel relaxed and refreshed and give you a

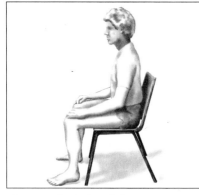

Fig. 1   *The Friendship Pose*

Fig. 2   *The Easy Pose*

Fig. 3   *The Auspicious Pose*

sense of purification. Meditation is easiest when your body is not preoccupied with digesting food, so it is best to meditate before eating, after a light meal, or several hours after a heavy meal. Also, one should avoid stimulants such as caffeine prior to meditating.

Loose, comfortable clothing is the most suitable for meditation. Tight, restrictive clothing and belts should be avoided or loosened. Remove glasses, watch bands, hard contact lenses or anything that puts pressure on your body. Remove your shoes. Because metabolism slows and the body cools off during meditation a warm shirt, sweater or a shawl draped over the shoulders can help to maintain warmth.

Some type of light exercise that loosens the muscles and creates physical relaxation is helpful. A few stretches or yoga exercises are good ways to release physical tension. A walk in the fresh air can clean out the lungs and loosen the limbs. Physical relaxation can be enhanced by lying down on your back and systematically releasing the tension from your muscles. Simply guide your attention through the major muscles groups directing them to let go and relax. Smooth, even breathing from the diaphragm will add to the physical relaxation and help prepare you for meditation. The underlying idea is that the body should be loose, relaxed and free of any tension that would only distract from meditation.

CHOOSING THE RIGHT POSITION

The actual position for meditation is important and should allow you to sit comfortably and steadily with the head, neck and trunk in alignment. Such a position allows for natural,

JOHN HARVEY, Ph.D

comfortable breathing. This type of posture is also the physical representation of an inner state of balance and alert attention that is an integral part of the meditative process.

The various meditative traditions have developed a number of postures which are ideal for meditation and which can fit different levels of flexibility and physical conditioning. The least demanding posture is aptly called the friendship pose. For this posture, you merely need to sit on the front part of a steady, firm chair. Place your feet on the floor about shoulders width apart, with the heels underneath the knees and the thighs parallel to the floor. Rest your palms on your knees or thighs (see figure 1). This is a very suitable posture and can be performed by a person of any age or any level of fitness.

Another very approachable posture is fittingly called the easy pose. This posture involves sitting on the floor and crossing your legs in front of you so that the left knee rests on the right foot and the right knee on the left foot. Place your palms on your knees. If you place a firm cushion or a folded blanket underneath your buttocks, you will reduce the strain on your legs and lower back and find it easier to align your head, neck and trunk. The easy pose is shown in figure 2.

The auspicious pose is somewhat more challenging and is best performed by those who are more limber. This pose is similar to the easy pose except that the legs are brought in closer and knees out farther, forming an even firmer and steadier base. While seated on the floor, bend the right leg at the knee and place the sole of the right foot against the left thigh. Bring the left ankle under the right ankle and position the sole of the left foot against the right thigh. Both feet should be positioned so that only the big toe is visible. Again, a firm cushion placed under the buttocks will make this position more comfortable and it will feel natural to align the head neck and trunk. The auspicious pose is seen in figure 3.

Once you select a pose for meditation, use it consistently so that your body becomes accustomed to the posture and you can gradually perfect it. Seated in a firm position you are ready to begin meditating.

HOW TO BEGIN

Bring yourself fully into the present by opening to the total experience of the breath.

Begin by gently closing your eyes so that your mind is not distracted by the sights around you and you can direct your attention inward. Take about five deep cleansing breaths. Start with an exhalation and push all the old stale air out by pulling in your abdominal muscles. Then relax the abdominal muscles and inhale deeply feeling the abdomen move out. Keep inhaling and filling the chest and finally, lift the shoulders to bring in additional fresh air. This breathing technique will leave you feeling refreshed and energized.

The next step is to achieve even, smooth diaphragmatic breathing. The diaphragm is a sheet of muscle between the lungs and the abdomen. The most efficient and relaxing breathing occurs when the abdominal muscles and diaphragm work in smooth coordination to bring in the most air with the least amount of effort. This type of breathing also leads the nervous system to a state of balance and creates a calm yet alert state that is conducive to meditation.

As you exhale, gently pull your abdominal muscles in. As you inhale, relax your abdominal muscles and feel the air being pulled deeply into your lungs. The exhalation is actually somewhat more active in terms of contracting the abdominal muscles and pushing the air out. The inhalation is more of an opening and relaxing, letting the air flow in.

Next, make your breath smooth and even. Notice any pauses, jerks, or jumps in the breath and gradually eliminate them. If your breath is noisy, let it become quiet. Make your inhalation and exhalation equal in length. Make the transitions between inhalation and exhalation smooth, without pauses or interruptions. Don't force the breath. Work within your comfortable capacity. With time and practice, it will become easier to establish smooth, even diaphragmatic breathing. Remember it is not something totally new you are learning. Every peaceful baby breathes in this manner and so at some level your body knows how to breath in this way. You simply have a lot of breathing habits that need to be changed.

Once the breath is flowing smoothly, scan your body systematically to reduce physical tension. Bring your awareness to your hands and fingers inviting and directing the muscles to relax. Then relax the arms and drop any unnecessary holding from the shoulders. Release across the chest, over the abdomen, down to the pelvis and the hips, the legs and down to the feet and toes. Then release any tension in the lower back, up the spine, around the shoulder blades, across the back of the neck, the back of the head and even the top of the head. Give special attention to the face which is the repository of so much emotional tension and mental striving. Smooth out the forehead, release any tightness from around the eyes, drop the holding in the jaw muscles and let your lips begin to form a smile.

FOCUS ON YOUR BREATH

Now you are ready to provide an object of focus for the mind and begin meditating. Bring your attention to your breath. Check to see that it is flowing smoothly and then begin to simply count the breath. Count one as you inhale and one as you exhale. Count two as you inhale and two as you exhale. Continue with this pattern up to ten and then start over. If you get distracted, and you will, then simply go back to one and start over.

Become fully aware of the experience of the breath as you count. With each number that you think, become aware of the rhythmic motion of the muscles of the abdomen and chest, feel the sensation of the air flowing through the nose and down to the lungs, and hear the subtle sound of the inhalation and exhalation. Sense yourself carried on the ebbing and flowing tide of the breath. Connect with the eternal rhythm of contraction and expansion. Bring yourself fully into the present by opening to the total experience of the breath. Let your mind stay focused on counting the breath.

This meditative technique may seem simple, but it can carry you to great depths of relaxation and tranquillity. The breath is an ideal object for meditation because it is ever present and rhythmical. It keeps awareness in the present. The counting of both the inhalation and exhalation is very useful for beginners and people with active, busy minds as it provides a more constant focus of attention.

Continue meditating for at least 10 to 20 minutes. Avoid pushing yourself beyond your comfortable capacity. When

Remember the effects of meditation are cumulative, so it is important to meditate daily even if it is just for a few minutes on a particularly busy day.

Whatever happens during meditation is fine. There is no such thing as a good or a bad meditation.

you first start practicing mediation, if you feel you have reached your limit, stop. As time goes on, you will find it easier to persist. Some people like to set a timer for 20 or 30 minutes so they don't have to think about the time and this can be useful. Remember the effects of meditation are cumulative, so it is important to meditate daily even if it is just for a few minutes on a particularly busy day.

When you finish meditating allow yourself time for a gradual transition back to a more active state. Open your eyes slowly. Take a moment to let your refreshed consciousness flow back out to the world around you. Sit quietly for a few minutes. Take a nice long stretch. Reflect on things. Take a few moments to read a paragraph or a page from one of the books on meditation listed in the resource section of this book. Then, when you are ready, resume your everyday activities keeping an element of mental relaxation with you.

There are several variations of this breath meditation. A traditional Zen format is to count just the exhalations up to ten and then start over. Slightly more advanced practitioners can simply focus fully on the breath without counting. This approach involves placing full awareness on the breath, on the inhalation and exhalation, on the tidal flow of contraction and expansion. However, of equal importance to the method of meditation is the manner and attitude with which the process of meditation is carried out.

Keep your full attention on the breath. Remember that meditation begins with concentration, but reaches its fullness when there is an unbroken flow toward the object of meditation, in this case, the breath. In order to deepen your concentration and create this unbroken flow, you will need to learn how to deal with distractions and how to cultivate certain helpful attitudes. Let us consider several of these attitudes first and then explore how they can help us to deal with distractions.

AN ATTITUDE OF NON-STRIVING

The first, and in some ways the most difficult attitude to create, is a spirit of non-striving. In modern western culture, we have accepted the assumption that results are linked to effort; the harder we work, the greater the results. However, the exer-

JOHN HARVEY, Ph.D

tion of effort is managed by the mind. When we are striving to accomplish something with meditation we end up stirring up more thoughts, feelings and physical reactions.

Meditation is all about quieting the conscious mind. As the mind is stilled, a great many things are accomplished. The nervous system moves to a state of balance and all of the bodily systems rest and actually repair and rebuild. The stillness of meditation allows us to access deeper levels of mind which nourish our spirit. In the case of meditation, less effort actually brings more results.

In a practical and positive sense, instead of struggling and striving to manage our thoughts we need to practice total acceptance, patience and a non-judgmental attitude. Whatever happens during meditation is fine. There is no such thing as a good or a bad meditation.

Acceptance means we accept whatever thoughts come to mind without judging them. The whole process of judging simply engages the mind and emotions. Try not to classify your thoughts as good or bad, just accept them. If you find yourself particularly distractable and unable to stay with the breath, accept yourself, and simply start over.

Patience refers to the understanding that meditation is not a sprint, but more of a marathon. So, we don't get excited when we experience a particularly peaceful meditation nor when we have a more chaotic meditation. We simply persist with patience. No matter how many times we find ourselves distracted, we patiently return our attention to counting the breath and start once again at one.

Working with the mind in the process of meditation is somewhat like training a young child. When a child misbehaves, we know it is not helpful to yell, scream and severely punish the child; this just creates more problems. Instead, with love, acceptance, patience and firmness, we guide the child in the proper direction. This is exactly what we should do with our mind when it wanders off during meditation.

As we develop the attitude of non-striving, we begin to experience an important dimension of the meditative process called witnessing. This means that we cultivate the ability to watch our thoughts without necessarily reacting to them. And it is this capacity to just witness the activity of the mind that slowly leads us to a state of quiet and balance.

Most of us live with the idea that we are inextricably bound to the content of our mind. Whatever images, memories and feelings cascade through the mind, we have to react to them, emotionally or analytically. The idea that we can just witness the activity of the mind without reacting, without getting caught up in our mental melodrama, is often a liberating revelation for the beginning meditator.

Witnessing can be strengthened by cultivating what is called mindfulness toward the activities of the mind. We can simply notice and label the current activity of the mind, and then gently return our awareness to counting the breath. Mindfulness helps us to eliminate the conflict of trying to do two things at once, i.e. focus on the breath and have some other feeling or thought. When we use mindfulness to acknowledge this other activity it brings us back into the present and clears the mind.

If a thought of the previous day emerges, we can acknowledge its presence as a memory. If a worry about tomorrow emerges, we can note it as such. If a feeling of frustration arises we can note it and even if a feeling of happiness arises, we can notice that as well. The best method is to tell ourself, "a feeling of frustration has arisen," let it go, and then return to the breath. Even if some feeling or thought persists, we can be mindful of that as well.

The key point is that we don't try to chase away, avoid or even appreciate any type of thought, feeling or perception. Nor do we engage in any analysis of it. We simply notice it, acknowledge it with present centered awareness, and let it go. As we are able to do this the mind will become more peaceful.

All of the above-mentioned attitudes will be quite helpful in allowing us to strengthen our concentration and move toward the uninterrupted flow of meditation. But surely we will experience distractions, and it will be useful to understand these, and know how to deal with them.

DEALING WITH DISTRACTIONS

One of the most common distractions is the sensation of discomfort in the body such as an aching muscle or joint, an itch or even a strong urge to move. Most of these distractions can be taken care of through proper preparation and position. If you have a lot of these physical distractions you may want to devote a little extra time to loosening and stretching exercises before you meditate. Taking a brief walk beforehand may also help to loosen the joints and muscles. Sometimes physical discomfort is caused by assuming a meditation posture that may demand more flexibility than you have at present. Accordingly, you may want to use a less demanding position.

Sometimes physical discomforts are more of a manifestation of mental restlessness, as the mind seizes on some minor sensation and magnifies it. In such instances practicing mindfulness and returning your focus to the breath may allow the discomfort to evaporate. Some sensations of discomfort may persist and require great mindfulness. Sometimes it may be advisable to avoid a major struggle with yourself and just scratch the itch or move the aching leg and then return your awareness to the breath.

A more dramatic distraction is some type of strong emotional reaction. You may sit down to meditate and find yourself vividly reliving an argument or confrontation that you had with someone that day. As soon as you close your eyes you see a constant replay of the incident and you feel all of the emotional upset and physical activation that accompanied the incident. You may feel that it just isn't worth it to meditate. But in fact this may be a good time to meditate.

Obviously you need to call on your witnessing skills and watch the incident without becoming involved. You need to expand your awareness of the breath, and notice as many dimensions of it as you can, such as the feeling of the abdominal muscles moving, the sensation of the air as it passes into the nose and down into the lungs, and even the subtle sound of the breath. This expanded awareness will bring you more into the present and out of the past.

Another method you can use to manage a strong emotional state is called cultivation of the opposite. If you feel anger towards someone, cultivate feelings of love and appreciation. If you feel sadness, dwell on an image of joy. If you feel envy, contemplate giving and sharing. Our mind seems to only have the capacity for one strong feeling at a time and so after a few minutes of cultivating the opposite, you may be balanced enough to return your awareness to the breath.

Sometimes we are even distracted by more positive experiences. This is especially true for creative and idea-productive personalities. As the mind is calmed we may find innovative ideas and creative solutions for problems streaming into our consciousness. One thought leads to another and before long we have created a new product, started a business, built a house, decorated a room, sewn a quilt or written a book all in our mind, and meanwhile the breath is left far behind. You can safely let go of these good ideas as well. If you thought of them they are yours. They will come back again when and if you need them. Learn to regard these "great ideas" with the same equanimity that you view the more negative reactions. Once again, return your awareness to the breath.

Another source of distraction can be the emergence of vivid memories. These are often quite compelling, creating strong emotional reactions, and an urge to analyze the memory. Actually, the emergence of memories may be a sign that meditation is beginning to cleanse and purify the mind. The memory was probably registered with a strong emotional reaction. If we are able to witness the memory and be mindful toward its contents, this strong reaction will be dissipated, the mind cleared and greater depths of meditation will be possible.

Anytime you have dealt with a distraction and are returning your focus to the breath, it is a good idea to recheck your posture and make sure your head, neck and trunk are properly aligned. Make sure that no unnecessary tension has crept into your neck and shoulders. Also give some attention to your facial muscles and to your breath. The impact of distractions is often recorded in patterns of facial tension and disruptions in the flow of the breath. Smooth out the face and by all means recreate that beginning smile. Re-establish smooth, even diaphragmatic breathing.

PERSISTENCE

As mentioned above the benefits of meditation are cumulative. The longer we practice, the more profound the influence on our physical and emotional health. Therefore, it will be useful to consider the means by which we can encourage regular meditative practice.

From a learning perspective, we know that behaviors can be strengthened by their consequences. If the consequences involve either an increased positive result or a decreased negative result the behavior will be strengthened. In this regard, meditation has built-in potential to become a consistent behavior because it is at once a pleasant, relaxing experience and it simultaneously reduces painful and harmful tension. Thus, if we practice meditation carefully, following the steps described in the preceding sections, and we open ourselves up to the experience, it should create a momentum that will help to sustain the practice.

In this context, it is important to make meditation enjoyable and not cast it as one more task added to our daily list. Select a pleasant spot for your mediation. Invest in a nice firm supportive cushion and a comfortable shawl. Choose a quiet and pleasant time of day. Life has many dimensions, but one of them is to enjoy the present. Meditation is one of the finest ways to enjoy the present.

Meditation: A Powerful Tool in the Clinic

Applications of meditation are becoming increasingly common in clinical settings. Perhaps one of the most successful applications has been Jon Kabat-Zinn's work with mindfulness meditation to treat patients suffering from chronic pain syndrome.

Chronic pain has long been one of the most difficult medical conditions to treat. Over time, pain medications lose their effectiveness and can lead to addiction. Chronic pain sufferers are less active, become deconditioned and fall into a cycle of increasing dependency and depression.

Kabat-Zinn provides chronic pain patients with a ten-week course in meditation, stress reduction and relaxation. The meditation helps patients to let go of their pain to access their natural healing resources, to accept themselves, and to enhance their coping skills. Meditation also helps patients to experience true peace of mind beyond their physical state and to initiate a process of growth based on a renewed personal vision.

Kabat-Zinn's research has shown that pain patients going through his program experience reductions in pain, in negative body image, depression and anxiety. They also decreased their use of pain medication and increased their activity levels. Most graduates of the program continued to meditate regularly and 15 months later were maintaining their improvements.

Meditation also appears to help people cope with the stress of everyday living. In a research project comparing the thinking styles of meditators and non-meditators, Duncan Currey found that meditators have a very characteristic cognitive coping style. They tend to be able to witness stressful events without always reacting to them. They are able to shift their attention away from the stressful event and toward their breath, which acts to center them. Meditators are more likely to arrive at a positive appraisal of stressful events. They also tend to see themselves as more relaxed in the face of stress. All of these thought patterns help to buffer individuals against the harmful effects of stress.

Changing your old routine is not always easy. A measure of commitment and self-discipline is needed. Clearly, in today's hectic, fast-paced world the need to relax, care for and nourish our minds must be seen as a priority. Possibly, in earlier times where life proceeded at a slower pace, there were natural opportunities to rest the mind. But now we need to create those opportunities. We simply must make a commitment to meditation as a priority in our life, a foundation upon which our well-being is built.

One useful way to make a commitment is on a trial basis. You can tell yourself that for one month you will get up 30 minutes earlier to make time for meditation. This is often much easier than making a lifelong commitment. Once the routine is established, it will be easy to maintain, particularly if meditation is enjoyable and beneficial. In fact most people who make such a commitment find that meditation is a wonderful way to start the day. And they notice that due to the meditation they actually require less sleep.

A tense mind can miss crucial details, and fail to see the big picture.

Inspiration is also important in sustaining a regular practice of meditation. Reading the thoughts and teachings of the masters of the meditative tradition can be very inspiring. Their teachings are typically based on their own practical experience and speak to us in a personal way. A number of books that provide this inspiration can be found in the resource list given at the end of this book. Reading and re-reading these books will help give you energy and strength to persist with your meditative practice. You will also learn additional breathing and meditative techniques to deepen your practice.

Another helpful source of inspiration is association with like-minded individuals. Even though meditation is ultimately an individual practice, contact with other people who are regular meditators can be encouraging and help to strengthen your practice.

Adjustments in your lifestyle can help your meditative practice. Drugs, alcohol and caffeine tend to stir up the mind and most meditators find that they prefer the natural refreshment and serenity of meditation to any chemically-produced state. A healthy diet with adequate whole grains, fresh fruits and vegetables and reduced sugar, fat and preservatives can make the mind clearer and facilitate meditation. A regimen of regular exercise can also be quite helpful.

Most of the meditative traditions also stressed the importance of certain attitudes toward life. These attitudes are designed to reduce the social and mental turmoil in our life which disturbs our meditation. Foremost among these principles is that of *ahimsa* or nonviolence, or cultivating a loving, accepting attitude toward all living beings and eschewing violence in thought, word and action. Another guideline is that of right work or doing work that is not exploitive or destructive. Nonviolence and right work are examples of principles that can help to make our lives more peaceful, our consciences clearer, and thereby help our meditative practice.

POSSIBILITIES

While meditation is the best method for relaxing the mind it also has possibilities for additional positive changes in the realms of personal effectiveness, personality integration, and self actualization. Let us briefly examine each of these realms:

Personal effectiveness is enhanced because we are taking care of that inner instrument, the mind. A mind that is rested and relaxed can more clearly focus on important activities. Sustained concentration is one key to productivity. The person who meditates continually expands his or her powers of concentration.

Meditation also leads to clear, unbiased perception. A tense mind can miss crucial details, and fail to see the big picture. A relaxed and rested mind can capture both. The mind that has been cared for is also likely to show more flexible problem solving, better deductive thinking and greater creative intuition. A relaxed mind simply has more energy to devote to a project.

Effectiveness in daily living can be further enhanced by the practice of meditation in action, which means maintaining an awareness of the breath while performing everyday activities. As we mow the lawn, talk on the phone, cook a meal or close a business deal, we can keep a certain amount of awareness on the breath. This keeps our experience in the present, allows us to witness our mental activity, and maintains contact with a sense of serenity and balance. Meditation in action allows us to

Meditation on the Job

An odd thing happens almost every day at the consulting firm Symetrix in Lexington, Mass. Some of its 125 workers shut their office doors, hold their calls, and spend 20 minutes sitting quietly, meditating.

They began doing this after going through a four-week program in which an instructor from Harvard's Mind/Body Medical Institute taught them a variety of techniques for relaxation, including meditation and guided visual imagery. George Bennett, Symetrix's CEO, says he signed up his company for the $3,000 program because employees complained of being too stressed out. "There's no question employees who do this are more relaxed, and some are even more productive," he says.

—From "Meditation, The New Balm For Corporate Stress,"
Business Week, May 10, 1993

refresh our mind on an ongoing basis. This practice adds depth and richness to every experience of daily life.

Meditation is also a method of personality integration. Witnessing and mindfulness help us to expand self knowledge. We observe our unique patterns of reactions and our characteristic thoughts. This expanding self awareness occurs in a non-judgmental and accepting context. The effect is quite therapeutic. Conflicts are eased and natural self esteem is increased.

Meditation also helps us to discover deeper dimensions of the self. When the conscious mind is stilled, the true self emerges. Each of us has a true nature, an essence, a storehouse of creative potential that begins to express itself as the conscious mind is stilled. This true self brings with it a feeling of connection and a clear sense of purpose and direction in life.

KEEPING IT SIMPLE

This chapter has provided you with an introduction to the practice of meditation. As you read more about meditation you will realize there are many traditions, each with its own technical terms and meditation techniques. Much of this is useful, and you may encounter more advanced meditation and breathing practices. But keep in mind that the heart of meditation is elegantly simple, and based on experience. The best results are obtained with regular, enjoyable practice.

CHAPTER 2

Yoga

Lilias Folan

At the age of thirty, Lilias Folan, a Cincinnati housewife and mother of two sons, discovered yoga. That discovery changed the direction of her life, and enabled her to reach out to a broad public to similarly improve their lives. The simple breathing and stretching techniques she learned (initially to relieve some minor ailments) became a powerful force for Lilias. Alive with new vitality and zest for life, she went on to study yoga with some of the best teachers in Europe, India and America.

Lilias began sharing what she learned with her family and then by giving classes in her community. Four years later, "Lilias, Yoga and You" began nationwide broadcast on PBS-TV stations. The overwhelming response to her yoga instruction came from housewives and senior citizens, as well as executives, professional athletes, artists, poets—even members of Congress.

After twenty years of yoga instruction on PBS-TV, as well as her own popular books and video's, Lilias Folan is an acknowledged authority, and a well-known advocate of the joys and benefits of yoga practice; some refer to her as "the Julia Child of Yoga." As vibrant in mid-life as ever before, she remains active on all fronts. She shares her latest relaxation techniques in a set of three audiotapes, "Rest, Relax and Sleep... Relax with Lilias!" These tapes have been used by individuals as well as hospital stress-management and wellness programs.

*Y*ears ago, I went to my family physician with a litany of problems. I wasn't sleeping well, my back bothered me, I felt tired each day by mid-morning, and I sensed a little gloom cloud of discontent always over my head. The doctor checked me over and gave me a clean bill of health. But he did say to me, "Madam, you are suffering from a case of the blahs! Get involved with an exercise program." Now, that was quite advanced thinking for those days. He did not give me a pill, or a fatherly pat on the head. He recommended exercise!

So I began to think about my choices... Tennis? Too sweaty! Golf? Not enough patience! Then I read a book about yoga, and it piqued my curiosity. I wondered how stretching, breathing, and relaxation could help me to sleep better, soothe my aching back, and uplift my sagging spirits. The day I took the first step upon the yoga path was the day that one door closed and a new one opened. That door led to health on all levels: Body, mind and spirit. If you, too, are curious and want to take the first step, here are some practical suggestions on how to approach yoga and a twenty-minute series of yoga exercises geared specifically for relaxation and stress relief.

WHAT YOGA IS

When I'm asked, "What is yoga?," I find that it is easier to begin by answering what yoga is not. Yoga is not about tying your body into knots. It is not about lying on a bed of nails. Nor is it eating yogurt, although I happen to (and I love it)!

Yoga is an ancient and wise philosophy from India. I am comfortable with defining yoga as the science and study of the self. Although yoga is many thousands of years old, I am amazed at the many ways it is used today in modern stress management programs, sleep disorder clinics, and hospital wellness programs throughout the world.

Yoga is often described as a large tree with many branches. One of the tree's smallest branches is what I enjoy both to study and to teach... Hatha Yoga. Hatha Yoga is a series of different postures or *asanas*. When we practice yoga, it is as if the body receives a wonderful message from the inside out. Each posture moves or is held in different positions. When you release or finish a pose, blood flushes into tissue, organs, joints—feeding, nourishing, the whole body as well as removing toxins and debris that have built up in the body.

BREATH IS THE KEY

Breathing and relaxation techniques are at the core of our yoga practice. It is important to remember that breath, body and mind are intimately connected. When the mind is disturbed, the breath and body are affected. When the body is active, the mind and breath will reflect the activity. You can quiet the mind by quieting the breath. You can learn to quiet your breathing by focusing on the activity of breathing. Eventually, a long, slow exhalation can serve as a natural tranquilizer.

In order to breathe properly—for yoga and in all our activities—it is important to understand our own breathing patterns, and to learn to practice deep, diaphragmic breathing—what I call "belly breathing."

Abdominal Breathing

Watching my four-year-old grandson asleep is the perfect example of good belly-breathing technique. In deep sleep, his abdomen expands slightly like a balloon on the inhale, and flattens on the exhale. Unfortunately for all of us, once our infancy has passed, we begin to live more in the mind and emotions. As we make this shift, our breathing patterns shift accordingly.

Much has been written about the "fight or flight" response. Basically, this response occurs in nervous system when we become fearful, worried or angry, for instance. This physical response to life's tension and stress is experienced by all ages.

Think about the last time you felt fear. What happened to your breathing at that moment? Chances are, you held your breath. This not a negative thing. We need that supercharged "pop" of energy we get when we hold our breath to cope with the next situation. However, once the crisis is past, it is important to go back to the belly breathing of our childhood. This is an easy, fun skill that is incredibly valuable to calm the mind and to restore peacefulness and a deep sense of relaxation.

Begin by observing your own breathing patterns. With a little interest and practice, you can enjoyably change the rhythm of your breathing from one that produces tension to one that produces relaxation.

Why is yoga on the rise? Because stress is, too. These aren't flower on the mats. In the '80s, young urban professionals complemented their go-go lifestyles with health-club memberships: they carried their competitive edge into aerobics and sweaty weight work. It brought thinner thighs but little relief from daily pressures. Says yoga student Christina Pearsall, a 28-year-old New York court stenographer; "I was so stressed out from work that it was just more jarring to jump around to house music in an aerobics class." But with the new decade came new fears: many who thought their fast-paced careers were stressful now face the prospect of pink slips and know what stress really is. So they decided to relax. Stretch. Concentrate on their breathing.

—From "Om is Where the Heart Is," by Mary Talbot and John Schwartz, in *Newsweek*, February 6, 1994

The Sigh

The Sigh... A sigh and a yawn are but a few of our body's amazing little gifts. A sigh is what I call an "organic breath." We don't have to think about it happening. Unfortunately, we tend to stifle yawns and sighs because they are socially impolite. However, I want to encourage you to sigh many times today. A long sigh of relief. Let go. Sighing and yawning are our body's natural ways to let go of stress and tension. Go ahead! Right now! Open your mouth and heave a great long sigh of relief. Again. Enjoy!

Gaining an Awareness

Sit tall in your chair. Slide forward slightly, perhaps place a pillow behind your back. Now, place one hand, palm down, inward, over the navel, then place the other palm on top of it. Do not change your breathing for the next six breaths. Simply observe with your eyes closed... Belly expand... Belly contract... As you breath in... As you breath out.

Come to Know Your Long Exhalation

Now, open your mouth and take in a good, deep breath. Then blow it out completely. Again, repeat... Breath in... Now, blow it out... Feel how the belly flattens... Flatten it more... Squeeze out... Out... Now, lips closed, let the next breath flow in effortlessly through the nose. Can you feel the belly expand? Good!

Continue to sharpen your focus on the exhale. Squeezing firmly in belly area the last few seconds. To slow down the exhale even more, use the letter "Sssssss". On your next out breath, open lips and exhale the letter Ssssss as long as you possibly can. Pushing the stale air from the basement of your lungs. Breathe in, lips closed. Repeat at least three times. Adding the sound will give you resistance and strengthen your control and understanding of the breathing process. Return once again to your belly breathing thru nostrils... Eyes closed... Notice as you breath in... Belly expands... As you breath out, belly contracts... Practice belly breathing during non-stressful times. This practice is there for you to use after the stressful moment has passed.

A Complete Diaphragmatic Breath

BENEFITS: Two or three minutes of this breath is a time out from tension. Also great to do before getting out of bed in the morning... Repeat two or three times... Continue breathing through the nose, not the mouth... Fully exhaling creates a vacuum that automatically pulls IN a deep diaphragmatic breath. Now, exhale completely, pulling the navel area in at the end, then imagine that your inhalation is filling a balloon in your belly. Fill the balloon, all the way up to the collar bone... Then, let it go slowly, and feel the balloon slowly emptying as you exhale... Navel in, gently, the last few seconds of each exhalation. Continue complete breath for one to three minutes... will provide a calm oasis within.

A TWENTY-MINUTE RELAXATION SERIES

Before You Begin

• Find a comfortable, quiet place to practice. Wear comfortable, loose fitting clothes, feet bare.

• Inform your family that you are not to be disturbed for the next twenty minutes to 1/2 hour. Take the phone off the hook, close the door.

• If you must eat, do it at least one hour earlier, and eat lightly.

• Choose the content of your practice with an awareness of your needs. Postures that open the chest will energize, and are good for morning wake ups. Forward bends and twists are calming; they are particularly effective to end your practice, or in preparing for a night's sleep.

• Remember to rest in between poses. (Take a "thirty-second vacation.") Rest is an important component within a yoga practice session; it helps your body absorb and integrate the postures and breathing. Rest rejuvenates.

Special Health Problems

If you are recovering from surgery, suffer from heart trouble, high blood pressure, please consult your doctor or health-care practitioner. There possibly are some moves not recommended for you at this time. Take this book and and any audio cassette or video yoga program you are considering to your physician or health care practitioner's office, and ask for their advice and support.

The Practice of Yoga Asana

Yoga is practiced slowly and mindfully. This is one reason that all ages can participate healthfully. There are hundreds of different classical yoga postures, most with many enjoyable variations. For this book, I have chosen gentle warmups and classic yoga postures for the body that encourage relaxation, release tension and stress. Remember, this is a yoga sampler, a series of movements that should take no more than 20 minutes to complete. My book, *Lilias Yoga and Your Life* and my relaxation tapes contain a more extensive useful sharing of this subject.

How to Use Your Breathing

Once you have gained an awareness and some level of control over your own breath, you can use those skills in coordination with your movements. Generally, when you open your chest, (arching), you breathe in. When you close the body, (forward bends), you exhale out. Breathe through the nose, with the lips closed, unless otherwise instructed. Breathe slowly and rhythmically. Coordinate breath and movement as much as possible. Use the exhale as a release.

SEATED RELAXATION POSE

BENEFITS: Will increase your awareness of your own needs and make you more sensitive to your physical condition—the many processes going on within.

Begin by sitting comfortably in a chair. Close your eyes and scan the body passively from the inside out. Try not to judge anything you see. Each day, you are different.

Sit tall. By this, I mean focus on making your spine long. Point your tailbone toward the floor. Pull your shoulders down, starting from ears, and rest hands comfortably in lap, with arms hanging down.

TAKE A THIRTY-SECOND VACATION

BENEFITS: You can relax any time, anywhere. You can remain supple and relaxed.

In seated pose, eyes closed, breathe in and then exhale. On the exhale, imagine that worries and cares of the day drain from your brain, down the side of your neck like a rushing river, cascading over your shoulders, through the arms, elbows, wrists, (forming pools) pooling in palms, then flowing into the tributaries of your fingers, then out the finger tips, dissolving silently in the space around you. (You can also try this in a bathtub, in a car at a stop light, or on a crowded bus).

HEAD ROLLS

BENEFITS: Releases tension in neck and shoulders.

As you exhale, drop your head towards your chest. Inhale, and rotate your head to the right. Hold for two or three breaths, take a long exhale and let gravity pull your head closer to the right shoulder. Make both shoulders heavy, pull them down beginning at ears. Observe stretch on left side of neck. Hold for two or three breaths. On the next exhale, drop chin to chest, inhale and rotate your head left. Hold for two to three breaths, make shoulders heavy. Observe the stretch on right side of neck. Be aware of feeling the stretch rather than the movement of the head. **CAUTION**: Do not drop head back on to shoulders. This can cause upper neck soreness.

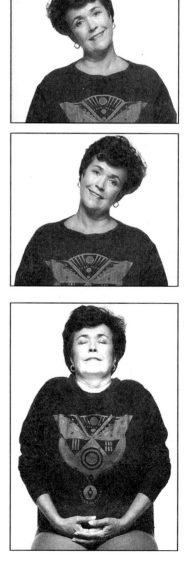

SHOULDER SHRUGS

BENEFITS: Releases the stress that collects in the muscles of the shoulders. Excellent to do anytime, anywhere.

As you inhale, shrug shoulders up under the ears. With a sigh, drop the shoulders. Let go! Exhale. Repeat two or three times. Really let go! Then shrug shoulders up, and then roll shoulder blades back and together. Repeat the shoulder rolls three to six times. Do not hold your breath. Observe your chest stretch open as you pull the shoulder blade together. **CAUTION**: Move within your comfortable range of motion.

Stretch and Yawn

BENEFITS: Releases tired, stale feelings in the body, gives you a "pop" of energy.

Sit tall, feet to the floor. On the inhale, raise both arms up to the ceiling, now stretch arms enjoyably. First one side then the other. Begin to yawn. Squeeze eyes closed. Comfortably open mouth. Give a good, long yawn sound ....AAAAAHHH. Stretch side to side. Repeat three times. Return to seated pose. Scan body, observe sensations within. CAUTION: Do not over-arch your lower back.

Back to Relaxation

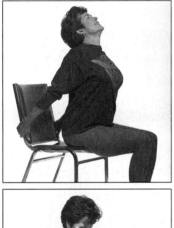

BENEFITS: Gently massages tight feelings of residual tensions held in the muscles of neck, back and chest.

Move to the edge of your chair. Sit tall, close eyes, place hands on chair or knees. Pay attention to inner sensations. Comfortably arch the spine, shrug shoulders up, lift breast bone, lift rib cage, lift chin, feel belly relax and expand. Pause, exhaling round the back, slide the hand forward to knees, roll the shoulders forward, contract the belly. With a sigh, let go. Repeat arch and release three times. Full attention to moving slowly, with the breath, the stretch, and now really let go with a good sigh, the letting go. CAUTION: Be sure that your back and neck are comfortable as you arch. The shrug should cradle and protect the neck as you lift your chin.

Knee to Chest *(Apanasana)*

BENEFITS: Increases circulation to the legs and to the inner organs of digestion and elimination. Releases tightness in the lower back. (This exercise is easy to do in bed before sleep and upon waking.)

Lie on back, knees apart and folded into the chest. Place hands over or under the knees. On the exhale, press the thighs to chest, very little effort in the arms. On the inhale, release. Repeat three to six times. Return to relaxation pose, close eyes, observe the sensations within the legs. CAUTION: Place hands under (not over) knees that are sore.

LITTLE BOAT *(Ardho Navasana)*

BENEFITS: Massages back muscles; soothing, restful effect.

Go into *Apanasana* (knees to chest), hands on or behind knees. Rock slowly from side to side like a little boat, nowhere to go, nothing to do. Just rock from side to side, right elbow to left elbow, breathing comfortably. As you roll right, turn head left.

THE SEED POSE (Restorative Side Relaxation)

BENEFITS: This is called a transition posture. It helps you move from one movement to the next in a restful way. The "Seed Pose" is a brief time to quietly reflect and absorb your practice, then move on to the next posture. By turning on your side before getting up, you are also caring for your back.

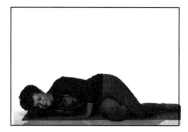

Lie on your side, place lower arm under head for pillow, upper arm in front of you, hand to floor. Bend both knees to chest. Rest, eyes closed for three to six breaths. Then lean forward, using upper hand to help push you up to a seated position.

SUN BIRD POSE *(Chakravakasana)*

BENEFITS: Helps to release and lengthen tight muscles of the torso. Massages inner organs behind the abdominal wall.

Body forms a table as you kneel on the floor or mat. Knees are comfortably hip width apart. Hands beneath shoulders, elbows soft. Hand are parallel. Head is slightly lifted, spine is long. Moving on the exhale, arch the spine, chin to throat.

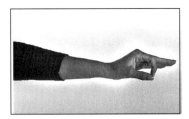

Moving on the inhale, slowly look up, arch in the other direction. Repeat three to six times. Inhaling, raise one arm up to the ceiling. Look up to raised hand. Exhale. Return to table, and repeat on opposite side. Join the thumb and fourth finger together. This is a signal for you to relax in this posture. CAUTION: Refrain from placing too much weight on your wrists. If wrists are sore, place elbows on mat.

RESTFUL CHILD'S POSE

BENEFITS: Passively relaxes muscles which stay tense without our knowing it.

Kneel and rest chest on your thighs. Place forehead on folded arms (or pillow, with arms alongside the body). For extra comfort, place a pad under knees and ankles. If buttocks don't rest on heels, place pillow beneath, then sit on pillow and heels. Inhale, into the abdomen, and into back. Exhale, visualize spine gently longer. Stay here as long as it is enjoyable, open thighs, feel your back lengthen. Adjust body, then rest again on your thighs. Sit up slowly. Move quietly into your next pose.

STANDING POSE *(Samasthiti)*

BENEFITS: This posture is a beautiful way to pause and collect yourself, and to endow this present moment with meaning. The past is finished, tomorrow has not yet arrived. Place the palms of hands together and BE in this timeless moment.

It is restful to breathe in as you slowly raise your arms, feel the chest open. Pause at the top. Exhaling, slowly lower the arms. Repeat three to six times. No rush. Feel the movement and the breath as one.

STRIDING FORWARD BEND *(Parshva Uttanasana)*

BENEFITS: A lively stretch for the whole body.

From a standing pose, stride right foot forward in a long step. Back foot is turned out 45 to 60 degrees. Begin with both legs strong and straight. If you feel off balance, move the right foot to the right, one inch. On the inhale, raise both arms up. Exhaling, fold your torso forward, palms resting on a chair seat, arms extended. Now soften right front knee. Hold for two or three breaths. Feel the back lengthen. Come up on one long inhale, first raise arms, then upper back, then lower back, then entire torso, up to a vertical position. Lower arms, repeat advancing left leg. As you progress, place hands lightly on floor instead of chair.

Variation: Using a chair (as illustrated at right) helps you to hold and enjoy the relaxation produced by this pose. CAUTION: Listen to your body. If needed, bend your elbows. Keeping the front knee soft is soothing and restful for your lower back.

THE WILLOW TREE *(Tiryaka Tadasana)*

BENEFITS: Excellent stretch for side muscles.

Begin in a standing pose, legs and ankles together like a strong and flexible willow tree. On your inhale, raise right arm up, place left arm on the shelf of lower back. Exhaling, stretch up then extend out into space left, (not down to floor). Return center, repeat opposite side. Return to standing pose. Close eyes, observe sensations within.

Variation: Left arm hangs heavily down. Hold for one to three breaths.

SEATED FORWARD BEND *(Maha mudra)*

BENEFITS: Considered one of the ten most important postures for centering scattered energy.

Sit on the floor, right leg straight, directly forward. Other leg is bent, left foot placed on the skin of inner thigh of straight leg. Turn torso so it is square over the right leg, chin to throat. Keep arms straight. Exhaling, fold torso forward and slide both hands under slightly-bent right knee. Inhale, return to center, Repeat, two or three times. Change legs, repeat two or three times.

Variation: Extend both legs out. Place hands on legs. Hold pose for two to three breaths. CAUTION: Please do not bounce. EXTEND on exhale. If you feel pain, consciously soften knees.

LYING DOWN TWIST *(Jathra parivritti)*

BENEFITS: As you twist water from a wash cloth, this posture gently "twists" out little aches and discomforts caused by stress held in the body. Twists have a calming effect on the nervous system.

Lie on your back, knees to chest, head centered, arms extended out from shoulders to form a "T". On the exhale, lower both knees eight inches to the right. Look over left shoulder. Hold for one to three breaths. Inhale, return to center. Repeat on opposite side. Repeat three to six times. As you progress, bring bent knee all the way to the floor. CAUTION: Open knees to release stress on lower back. Do not force knees or shoulders to floor. Keep your head facing center if you suffer from neck problems.

The Four Steps of Relaxation

The following four key steps will guide you into a deep state of relaxation.

FOCUS - SUGGEST - PAUSE - FEEL

FOCUS — Imagine that you can direct your inner focus, or concentration, like a beam of light. You are the lighthouse. Where you focus your mind, energy follows. When you are into the actual experience of relaxation, chances are that you'll observe that your mind wanders. There goes that monkey again. Please know that it is the nature of the mind to wander. Just bring it back, again and again. In time, with practice, you will experience your inner focus become strong and clear.

SUGGEST — We all have an internal dialogue that carries on within the mind, day and night. Now you can harness and redirect this energy, previously wasted in meaningless inner dialogue, and use it to help you relax. The "Suggestion" is a simple, clear command aimed at the part of the body that you are going to relax. YOU make suggestions all through the relaxation. (You) I (are) am (the) your guide. They are short and powerful. Know that your body is waiting to receive your positive internal words of guidance and healing.

"When the sea was calm, all the boats showed mastership in floating."

- Shakespeare

PAUSE — Each time you focus and then suggest a specific relaxation, such as, "my jaw muscle feels slack." Wait a moment. Pause. Allow your mind some space to listen, feel, and receive the sensations which come when the muscles relax.

FEEL — Relaxation is a feeling. Stress feels like something too, like a knot in the gut, a pain in the neck. Conversely, when the muscles relax, there are subtle feelings such as softness... heavy... smooth... tingling... warmth. The art of relaxation has kept my interest for over three decades. Why? Because each time I dive inwards, it is different. I feel and experience an inner landscape of color, light, shapes, feelings, memories, always different, always changing. Beneath it all is a dynamic stillness.

RESTORATIVE RELAXATION POSE
(*Sarvasana* or Sponge)

BENEFITS: This is your time to rest and restore on a cellular level, your own dynamic stillness.

Proper head preparation and neck support is so beneficial and effective for deep relaxation. It is worth your time and effort. Please do not short-change yourself by rushing through the following preparation.

You will need the following relaxation props:

- Three hand towels

- Two or three bath towels

- One bolster or pillow

- Strong rubber bands

When I have finished relaxing, I place all the props in a bag, ready to use again.

Carefully roll a hand towel (no wrinkles) into a neat roll that fits and supports your neck curve. Secure this roll with a rubber band around each end. Make the head pad and chest-support pad in the same careful way. Fold two hand towels for the head pad. Fold bath towels in thirds, then fold again in half. Make sure the towel is smooth, with no lumps. Lie down (on back) so that the edge of the chest support towel is just behind your waist. The bolster is beneath your knees. Place the neck roll behind neck, and the head pad towel beneath the head. Close eyes, and observe the nice open feeling in your chest. Bent knees release tension in lower back. Place arms along sides and slightly away from the body. Join thumbs and fourth finger, signalling to all systems... relax, rest, and restore. Now you are ready to go through the following, or you might enjoy listening to my relaxation tapes at this time.

ALERT RELAXATION
(Adapted from Yoga Nidra)

First, read these directions to yourself. Then you can read them to friend or into a tape machine, pausing a few seconds at each set of dots...

Focus your attention, like a beam of light, to where the heels touch... Inhale, stretch the toes wide apart... Hold the breath and feel the stretch... Exhaling, release the feet. Feel the sensation within each toe... Again, focus on feet, inhale, hold the breath and stretch both feet... Exhale, release, feel the sensation within the feet.

Focus your attention on right leg... Moving only on inhale, lift it six inches off surface... Pause... Exhaling, let the leg flop... Suggest, "my leg feels hollow."... Pause... Feel the sensation... Repeat on left leg... Move the beam of light upward... Focus on the buttock muscles... Inhaling, firmly contract buttock muscle like two rocks... Hold the tension for a few seconds... Then exhaling, let go... Pause... Feel the sensation of melting within the seat muscle... If you feel nothing, repeat. Take your time.

Focus on the right arm... Lift off the surface... Make a fist... Inhale... Tense the arm... Hold a few seconds... Release and exhale... Feel the sensations within arm as muscles relax... Pulsation? Heaviness? Compare the difference between the right hand and the left one. Be accurate... Repeat the left arm...

Focus on your face... Inhale... Hold the breath... Now make a prune face... Hold, feel the tightness... Squeeze face muscles in towards the nose... Exhale and let go... Pause, and feel the sensations that follow, the pulsations within your face.

Focus on forehead... Suggest, "Lines of my forehead smooth"... Pause... Feel forehead smooth as a silk scarf... Focus on your eye lids... Really feel where the two lids touch... Suggest, "my upper eye lids heavy."... Pause... Feel the eye lids heavy...

Focus on your two lips... Upper lip... Lower lip... Take your time, feel where two lips touch... let the corners of your mouth turn up...

Focus inside the mouth... Feel where tongue touches teeth... The moistness inside the mouth... Now go to the strong jaw hinge muscle... Suggest, "My jaw muscle slack."... Pause... Feel the sensation as the jaw muscle slackens...

Now focus your attention, like a beam of light, down to the chest... Do nothing... Just observe the chest rise on the inhale, and fall on the exhale... On your next exhalation, suggest, "My chest is heavy."... Pause to feel the bones of the chest sink into your surface... Repeat this command until you really feel the sinking, heavy feeling... Now relax all efforts... Rest and restore for a few minutes longer... Nowhere to go... Nothing to do... But watch your breathing flow in and out. When you are ready, turn on your side for the seed pose. Let this be the moment of transition. Take the calm, clear, relaxed feelings on with you into your day.

CHAPTER 3

Food for Relaxation

Annemarie Colbin, CHES

Annemarie Colbin, M.A., C.C.P., C.H.E.S., is founder and president of the Natural Gourmet Institute for Food and Health in New York. She has been teaching health-supportive cooking and natural healing techniques since 1972. Colbin is a syndicated columnist and author of *The Book of Whole Meals, Food and* *Healing, The Natural Gourmet* and the home video, *"Basics of Healthy Cooking".*

Colbin has appeared on numerous radio and television shows around the country and abroad, and she lectures widely. She is on the faculty of the New York Open Center and Omega Institute, and the Advisory Committee of the Manhattan Center for Living. Her column appears regularly in Free Spirit magazine. Colbin is the recipient of the Roundtable for Women in Foodservice 1987 Pacesetter Award in Education and the Avon 1993 Women of Enterprise Award.

*E*ating in itself can be relaxing, regardless of what is being eaten. Nevertheless, there are some foods that promote relaxation more than others, because of their effects on your brain and your energy.

The purpose of this chapter is to give you some pointers about both what you eat and how you eat, so as to enhance your ability to reduce stress and relax.

DEFINING OUR PARADIGMS

To understand each other, we need a common idea of how the world works, otherwise known as paradigm or mental model. This model is a concept and picture we carry around in our heads; we use it to figure out what happened, predict what's going to happen next, and make decisions. It also gives us a common language, through which we understand each other. For example, an old paradigm was that the world is flat; every body had that picture in their minds, and believed the prediction that if you went far enough you would fall off, so the decision was to stay close to home. When some rebels decided to check and found out that they didn't fall off, but came back home from the other side, the paradigm changed. With the mental model of a round world, travel became commonplace; nobody is afraid of falling off anymore.

In the area of health, every culture has its own paradigms. Because the cultural paradigm is to its people as water is to a fish, it is generally assumed to be "the Truth." In traditional cultures, for example, the paradigm can say that people get sick because they have been exposed to evil, invisible spirits; the medicine used in those cultures concerns itself with preventing or canceling out these negative energies. In our own culture, the paradigm is that people get sick because they have been exposed to nasty, invisible (to the naked eye) bacteria or viruses; the medicine we use concerns itself with eliminating those creatures. The more accurate the predictions, the better the paradigm.

The Nutritional Science Paradigm

Our own science presents a view of the world that is very interesting and sophisticated. It's a good idea to know it well.

It is also not the only way to look at things. Therefore, in this chapter, we'll briefly look at two paradigms: the scientific one, and a variation on the Chinese yin/yang theory.

In Western nutritional science, it is agreed that food is made up of nutrients, which include protein, carbohydrates, fats, vitamins and minerals. For our purposes, we are interested mostly in protein and carbohydrates. These two nutrients are instrumental in the manufacture and transport of the neurotransmitters, or brain chemicals, the chemical substances, made by the brain and other organs, that transmit thought. The main neurotransmitters for our purposes are the alertness chemicals and the calming chemicals.

Three of the many amino acids in protein contribute to making these neurotransmitters: tyrosine, phenylalanine, and tryptophan. The first two are involved in the building of dopamine, norepinephrine, and adrenaline; these are the "alertness chemicals," and cause us to be mentally energetic and alert. Tryptophan is the precursor to the brain chemical serotonin, which is the "calming chemical" and makes us more relaxed and calm.

Amino Acids and their Neurotransmitters

AMINO ACIDS	NEUROTRANSMITTERS
Tyrosine and Phenylalanine	Alertness chemicals: dopamine norepinephrine adrenaline
Tryptophan	Calming chemical serotonin

All the amino acids are present in the protein foods, and do their work when they're taken up by the brain. Because there are many different kinds of amino acids in natural foods, they compete with each other for access to the brain, thus preventing the tyranny of any single one with its inevitable imbalances. Among the three amino acids, tryptophan seems to be the laggard, and usually is last on the uptake by the brain ~ UNLESS it is consumed with a carbohydrate food such as sweets or starches.

When you consume a small amount of protein food, by itself, without accompanying carbohydrates, your brain will make more of the energizing brain chemicals. However, a large amount of protein foods does not adhere to this pattern, but instead creates the opposite: sleepiness and lethargy. When you eat a carbohydrate food with some protein (as in a grain and bean combination, or a chicken sandwich), the carbohydrate will stimulate the production of insulin which will allow for more tryptophan uptake by the brain, and create a calm and focused mood. If the carbohydrate is complex and comes with its natural complement of fiber, such as in whole grains, it can set up a steady mood of continuous energy: the fiber slows down the speed of nutrient absorption into the bloodstream, so insulin is released more gradually and the production of serotonin more measured. On the other hand, if you eat a large amount of low or no-fiber carbohydrate food, particularly white flour and simple refined sugar, without any protein around it, it may swing the pendulum too far and also create sleepiness and lethargy.

The Chinese Paradigm

In Chinese philosophy and medicine, the dominant paradigm states that all things in the universe are the result of the interplay of two opposing forces, one called yin and the other called yang. Health emerges naturally when both forces are in balance, with neither dominant. Illness happens when the two are out of harmony in the body. Imbalance can occur when there is too much or too little of either side of the pair; interestingly enough, going to either extreme brings out the opposite force. It is our nature, as creatures of nature, to continuously create balance by swinging from one to the other.

For the purpose of clarity, instead of the words yin and yang, I'll use a set of opposites that operates all through the body: expansion/contraction. For example, our lungs expand and contract, our heart does the same, and so do all our blood vessels and hollow organs like the stomach, gallbladder, and intestines.

Expansive/Contractive Food List:

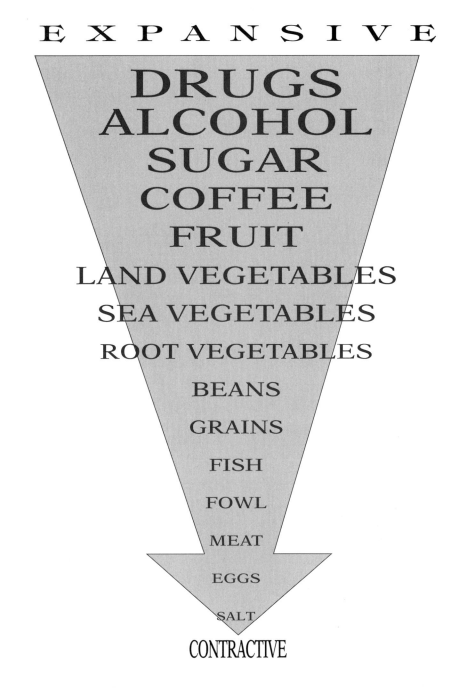

EXPANSIVE

DRUGS
ALCOHOL
SUGAR
COFFEE
FRUIT
LAND VEGETABLES
SEA VEGETABLES
ROOT VEGETABLES
BEANS
GRAINS
FISH
FOWL
MEAT
EGGS
SALT

CONTRACTIVE

The pendulum of our energy swings from one to the other. For good health, there must be a comfortable balance between the two. Excess of either is counterproductive. Too much contraction, and we're uptight, tense, rigid; Enough contraction, and we can concentrate and focus. Too little, and we lose our center. Too much expansion, and we get "spaced out." Enough expansion, and we are comfortably loose and relaxed. Too little, and we get stuck, we need to loosen up.

Tension can be classified as contractive; relaxation can be considered expansive. The foods you eat may have an "expansive" or "contractive" effect on how the energy moves in the body, and affect your physiology as well as your energy. A symptom or mood of one kind can be counterbalanced with a food of the opposite kind.

The foods on the extremes of this chart (drugs, alcohol, sugar, meat, salt) tend to have dramatic effects that initially feel good, but when used daily and often they tend to create habituation: the opposite feelings of unhappiness and discomfort emerge, and these make us require even more of the stimulants for the same pleasurable effect. In the long run, the extremes will create disturbances in our health. Intelligent moderation is, as always, the key to success.

HOW CAN FOOD CONTRIBUTE TO TENSION?

It is not farfetched to suggest that the food and drink you consume can make you more tense. Among the main culprits:

STIMULANTS AND CAFFEINE   Present in tobacco, coffee, tea, chocolate, colas. Even decaffeinated coffees and teas have traces of this alkaloid! These substances first seem to expand you, and create alertness and energy; yet when used to excess they tighten you up and bring on tension. Any attempt to defuse the tension by having some more coffee or chocolate only makes things worse.

ALCOHOL AND SUGAR   These first relax you and then cause sleepiness. However, because they're on the extreme of the scale, they have some peculiar effects. Alcohol use, which affects the liver, in the long run brings out the opposite and makes people tense and angry. Some people with weak immune systems react to sugar with an onslaught of serontonin that creates the famous "sugar rush," a sense of being high, highly alert and clear—quite the opposite of relaxation.

Goodbye to the Tension Headache

The greatest enemy of relaxation is that awful feeling of tightness around the temples, along the back of the neck, the upper part of the shoulders. If you were to look up that trajectory on an acupuncture meridian chart, you'd notice that it follows the meridian of the gallbladder. The meridians of Chinese acupuncture are invisible channels along which our life energy (chi) flows; when the energy is blocked, imbalance occurs first, and if not corrected, eventual illness may develop. I always find it illuminating to check the meridian point whenever there is pain, or I bang myself into something (that's natural or unconscious acupuncture!).

The liver and gallbladder have to deal with, among many other things, our intake of fats. The more fats in the diet, the harder those organs have to work. When they get overworked, tired, sluggish, congested ~ pain arises along the meridians. Hence, a high-fat diet, or even just one high-fat meal, could set the stage so that when psychological stress and tension occur, they are felt along the gallbladder meridians.

Therefore, the number one dietary caveat to avoid tension headaches:

• Keep your oil and fat intake low: no fried foods, easy on the salad dressing, watch the butter, omit the sauce Alfredo, the pesto, the mayonnaise (as in tuna or chicken salad), the fatty meats and cheeses. Take it easy on the milk products as well.

As alcohol also is metabolized in the liver, here is number two:

• Keep yourself to one glass of wine with dinner, or half a beer per evening.

If, through no fault of your own, the headache has struck already, there are some easy ways to eliminate it. First, classify it under the contractive category. Therefore, counterbalance it with expansive elements. The most healthful of these are:

• About two cups at a clip of any of the following: Cold and sweet/sour fruit juices (apple, orange, apricot, pear, peach, unsweetened grape); seltzer or mineral water with lemon; vegetable juices without salt, with some extra lemon.

Once the headache is on the way out and your appetite returns, have dinner:

• A light meal with lots of steamed vegetables, salad with lemon (no oil), steamed brown rice, poached or broiled fish. Or simply just some fruit (all the better if organic). To complete the cure, have a good shiatsu massage.

Quick Relaxers

Judith Wurtman, Ph.D, a well-known researcher at the Massachusetts Institute of Technology, was one of the first to bring the neurotransmitter theory to the public, with her book *Managing your Mind and Mood through Food*. She pointed out that the quickest way to relax is to eat a carbohydrate with no protein. Among the carbos she recommends are air-popped popcorn, rice cakes, and dry breakfast cereals without milk.

In her fine books *The Food Pharmacy* and *Food: Your Miracle Medicine*, Jean Carper mentions the following associated with stress, tension, anxiety, and mood swings.

Coffee and alcohol:

Both of these commonly used substances may cause anxiety or panic attacks.

Selenium:

Foods high in selenium may improve moods, such as sunflower seeds, oysters, swordfish, or clams.

Onion:

Used by the ancient Egyptians to induce relaxation and sleep, yellow and red onions are mild sedatives.

The expansive/contractive, or yin/yang, system, has been popularized mostly by the macrobiotic movement. In *Macrobiotic Home Remedies*, by Michio Kushi, the following are recommended for calming and relaxing:

Kombu tea:

Boil one 3" strip of kombu seaweed in 1 quart of water for 10 minutes.

Shiso leaves:

These are most easily found in a jar with whole pickled plums (umeboshi). Simmer them in water to make a tea, which is also helpful for indigestion or food poisoning.

Cooked onions:

In soups or vegetable dishes. A traditional Japanese folk remedy for insomnia consists in placing a cut raw onion under the pillow!

However, what goes up must come down; the high becomes a low, and eventually, they feel not just relaxed, but tired and exhausted all the time. All of these are different gradations of expansiveness.

ANIMAL PROTEIN   When used in small amounts of 2 to 3 ounces per meal, protein energizes initially by stimulating the alertness chemicals, dopamine, norepinephrine, and adrenaline. When used in larger quantities and several times a day, it creates tension and hardness, which then require alcohol and sugar to break them up; the final result is either a "Type A" behavior, or listlessness and lethargy.

How Can Food Help You Relax?

By now you have probably figured this out by yourself. Food helps you relax by bringing in expansive energy to counteract the contraction of tension, and by stimulating the relaxing brain chemical serotonin. Sweets and carbohydrates will do it; however, refined sugar and white flour, while they fill the bill in terms of carbohydrates, are not the best choices because they are missing most vitamins and minerals that you need. Here are the best foods to go for when you need to wind down and loosen up:

- Juices and fruit instead of alcohol.

- Complex carbohydrates with fiber: Whole grain bread, whole wheat, pasta, oatmeal, brown rice, quinoa, polenta, popcorn, grits, and so on.

- Indian food, mild vegetable curries, desserts flavored with aromatic spices such as cloves, cinnamon, nutmeg.

- Sweets made with natural sweeteners such as maple syrup, barley or rice malt, fruit concentrates, jams and jellies made with pure fruit.

Note that the carbohydrates promote calmness, relaxation, and eventually sleepiness. For that reason, you may want to reconsider your habit of having something sweet for breakfast: you may need lots of extra coffee during the morning just to counteract the serotonin-enhancing carbohydrates. Relaxation is good, but not when you're supposed to be doing a high-powered presentation to your major client! Try something with protein (how about a piece of fish, smoked or broiled, with dark rye bread, like the Northern Europeans have?) If you need to scarf down something from a coffee shop, try the English muffin, rye toast, bagel, or oatmeal, rather than a muffin which is usually high in sugar.

HOW TO EAT OUT WHEN YOU'RE RUSHED AND CAN'T AFFORD TO STOP

One of my students said she likes to have a blender drink for breakfast, because she won't sit down to eat. I asked her how does she down the drink, sitting or standing; she said standing, because she is too rushed to do otherwise. My suggestion to her, and to others who feel similarly, is to eat a healthy, high fiber breakfast ~ standing up, or even walking about! You can move your arms and legs, walk, clean, finish your grooming rituals ~ all the while chewing on some good sourdough bread, or a mouthful of oatmeal, or an egg sandwich on rye toast.

In our exciting and busy lives, eating is usually a low-priority activity. We seem to have developed a certain disdain for it. And yet eating is a major survival tactic: if we don't eat, we die. It's as simple as that. Nevertheless, many of us go rushing about and "just grab something" that's near, easy, or cheap. I maintain that it is possible to "grab something" with a certain amount of planning and intelligence, so that we don't shoot ourselves in our nutritional foot. Here are some basic ideas for "grabbing something" on the run, offered by someone who lives in a big city where there are three food establishments per block; in suburban and rural areas, you may have to get inspired and develop your own practical strategies.

COFFEE SHOPS OR DELIS   Rye toast or bread, bialy, English muffin, bagel; plain, with a smidgen of butter. Sandwiches: sliced turkey, turkey or chicken breast, roast beef (these are low in fat; skip the tuna and chicken salad with their gobs of mayonnaise). Soups: anything with beans or legumes, such as split pea, lentil, yankee bean, or black bean soup, as well as vegetable and chicken soups. In fact, a hearty bean or chicken soup with bread is a great, light meal, low in fat and cholesterol, and with enough protein and minerals in it to keep you energized during a rushed period.

OTHER ESTABLISHMENTS   Falafel or gyro, egg roll, steamed dumplings, hoagie with lots of salad and little meat, and so on. Sometimes, when eating out, it's very hard to avoid

When McDonald's established a beachhead in Rome's Piazza Navona three years ago, wine and food writer Carlo Petrini declared war. Concerned that the onslaught of fast food threatened Italy's gastronomic heritage, he counterattacked with The Slow Food Foundation, dedicated to eating slowly and savoring the moment. Membership mushroomed in Italy and 26 other countries. Now the war has come to burgerland.

In the past month, 10 chapters or *convivia*, have sprung up in the United States from New York to San Francisco. "We believe fast food is an impoverishment to the culture," says U.S. president Flavio Accornero, a New York wine merchant. "Doing things quickly is against our basic philosophy." For a $55 fee, members receive national and international newsletters, a wine and food encyclopedia, and a silver pin of their mascot—a snail. Besides promoting American cuisine, Accornero hopes to revive discourse along with the three-course meal: "That's the only time we have to get together and talk."

—From "Fast Food, Slow Down!," by Jeanne Gordon, in *Newsweek*, May 21, 1994 the fat, but try to minimize it, and accompany with fruit juice or seltzer with lemon to help in the digestion.

AT HOME   Mashed avocado with a little salsa on whole wheat pita bread, hard-boiled egg (keep yourself to two eggs per week, just to be safe; make sure they're organic or free range, they taste much better). A great low-fat snack food, and a very relaxing one, is a baked yam. To have them at hand, put six yams (sweet potatoes) in a 400 oven for one hour; do not wrap or puncture the skin. Keep them in the fridge, and use either cold, or sliced and steamed, grilled or pan fried.

Remember, if you need alertness and energy, you want to focus on the protein. Pasta and salad for lunch will tend to make you relaxed or tired at a time when that may not be what you want; try fish or chicken and salad, stir-fried vegetables with shrimp or scallops, or any other form of protein at lunch, and no dessert.

Notice I don't recommend a piece of cheese or a yogurt. That is because in my experience many people feel better, lighter, and less congested when they avoid milk products. Therefore I prefer to suggest a dairy-free regime.

Eating to Unwind

Here's where the carbohydrates come in; still, keep an eye on your fiber intake. It may be a bit tricky eating out, but it can be done, especially in the better restaurants. Choose among the following: pastas, polenta, rice dishes, cooked vegetables, salads, curries, baked or broiled fresh fish, and any of the traditional ethnic dishes that are low in protein and high in the complex carbohydrates. If you're choosing a meal with some animal food in it, as in a French restaurant, have one glass of wine; one will relax, but more is likelier to cause a pendulum swing of tiredness and headache the next day. Avoid alcohol with vegetarian and low-fat meals; it seems to have a much stronger effect in that context. If you're going to have dessert, try a fruit-based one, or one with as little sugar as possible. Stay away from chocolate, which is a stimulant.

If you do any kind of cooking, aim for a high-fiber vegetarian dinner at home, both to relax and to insure your basic nutrition. Go for brown rice, barley, polenta, kasha (buckwheat), and soup with white beans or lentils in it, some green vegetables like broccoli or collard greens, baked yams or squash. This is also the appropriate time to have dessert, preferably sweetened with a natural sweetener such as maple syrup, barley malt, or fruit juice.

Here is an easy and relaxing meal to make at home. Put on your most comfortable clothes, go barefoot if you like, turn on some good music (not too loud!), and get into the kitchen.

Dinner

Simple Lentil Soup
Herbed Polenta
Sauteed Portobello Mushrooms with Garlic
Mesclun Salad with Balsamic Mustard
*   Vinaigrette*
Vermont Bananas

Simple Lentil Soup

1 cup lentils
4 cups spring or filtered water or stock
*   (vegetable or chicken)*
1 small onion, diced
1 tsp. extra virgin olive oil
1 carrot, diced
1/2 green pepper, diced
1 bay leaf
1/2 tsp. sea salt, or to taste
freshly ground pepper to taste
chopped chives or parsley

1 Place the lentils in a 2 or 3-quart saucepan; add cold running water from the tap until well covered, swirl them around, then pour off all the water with whatever is floating in it. If the lentils are very dirty, repeat. Then add the 4 cups water or stock, bring to a boil, cover, reduce the heat to low, and simmer for 30 minutes while you prep the vegetables.

2 In a sauté pan or skillet, heat the oil, then sauté the onions for a minute or so; add the carrot and green pepper, stirring each time. Pour all into the soup pot; with a ladle, scoop some stock into the skillet while still hot, swirl around, to pick up all the flavoring, and return to the soup pot. Add bay leaf. Cover, and simmer another 30 minutes. Add salt ten minutes before the end of cooking.

3 Place about a cup or two of the soup in the blender, and puree; then return to the pot. Adjust to taste. Serve hot with freshly ground pepper, garnished with chives or parsley. Makes six servings. Keeps well for 4-5 days in the refrigerator.

Herbed Polenta

3 cups unsalted chicken stock, vegetable stock, or water
1/2 tsp. sea salt or to taste
1/2 tsp. each dry oregano and basil
1 cup yellow corn grits or coarse corn meal (organic if possible;
*   try Arrowhead Mills brand)*
dash of Tabasco or hot sauce, to taste

1 In a heavy saucepan, bring stock or water to a boil with the salt and herbs, then whisk in the grits or corn meal. Stir continuously until thick. Cover, and simmer 30 minutes, stirring often.

2 Just before serving, add the Tabasco or hot sauce. Stir well. Serve hot straight out of the pan, with a large serving spoon, making a mound on the plate. The polenta can also be poured into a shallow baking pan or a loaf pan and allowed to cool and set. If in the shallow pan, it can be cut into rectangles or shapes, and if in the loaf pan, it can be cut into slices; these can then be fried on each side, or brushed with oil and baked or broiled until heated through. Makes 4 servings.

Sautéed Portobello Mushrooms with Garlic

4 cloves garlic, minced
1 tbsp. extra virgin olive oil
2 large (5-6") Portobello mushroom caps, wiped with
damp cloth or paper towel, cut into 1/2" chunks
1/4 tsp. sea salt
1/4 tsp. freshly ground pepper, or to taste

1 In a large skillet, heat the oil, add the garlic, stir for a minute, then add the mushroom chunks. Sprinkle salt and pepper all over. Stir or shake to flip frequently. Cook until the mushrooms are shrunk and almost black (not burned, just changed color), about 10 minutes. Serve hot atop the polenta. Makes 4 servings.

Mesclun Salad with Balsamic Mustard Vinaigrette

1/3 lb. mesclun mix, baby greens or mixed salad greens
1/2 small red onion, sliced thin
1 tbsp. balsamic vinegar
3 tbsp. extra virgin olive oil
1 tsp. prepared whole-grain mustard, such as Pommery

1 Place the salad greens in a large bowl, add the onions slices.

2 Combine all dressing ingredients in a bowl or jar, then whisk or shake well to blend. Drizzle evenly over the greens, toss and serve. Makes 4 servings.

Bananas Vermont

4 bananas, ripe but firm
1 tbsp. unsalted butter
1 tbsp. maple syrup
2 tbsp. water

1 Peel the bananas, and cut them once in half across, then each piece in half again lengthwise.

2 Melt the butter, and pour into a 9x14" baking pan. Arrange the bananas in it, turning once to get a little butter on the other side.

3 Mix the water and maple syrup, and drizzle over the bananas. Broil for 5 minutes, or until the bananas soften. Serve 4 pieces per person. Makes 4 servings.

To relax and enjoy your meal to the fullest, chew each mouthful until the food is completely puréed, and pay attention to the depth and the changing of the flavors.

Relaxing Foods and Drinks

My very favorite anti-stress remedy is the following. Many of my students swear by it, both as a relaxer as well as for relieving insomnia. Kuzu is a chunky white powder, obtainable in health food stores; it's extracted from the root of the Japanese kudzu plant, and has a fair amount of calcium, which helps relax the nervous system. Coupled with the hot, sweet carbohydrate of the apple juice, it has a dramatic relaxing effect. For the best results, have it before bed.

Apple Juice Kuzu Pudding

1 cup unfiltered apple juice
2 1/2 tbsp. kuzu powder
1/2 tsp. vanilla extract
1 tbsp. tahini (sesame butter) (optional)

1 In a small saucepan, mix the kuzu with the cold apple juice until dissolved. Add the vanilla.

2 Heat over a medium-high flame, stirring continuously, until it comes to a boil and thickens. Remove from the heat; swirl in the tahini, and serve immediately. Makes 1 or 2 servings. For the fat-free version, omit the tahini.

If you can't find the kuzu, try the following.

Hot Apple or Pear Juice with Cinnamon

1 cup unfiltered apple or pear juice
1 cinnamon stick

1 Heat the juice, with the cinnamon stick, over medium heat until just below boiling. Do not boil. Drink immediately. Makes one serving.

When the weather is hot, and you're ready to sit down and relax, try some of these:

Frozen Banana Ice Cream

2 ripe bananas, peeled, cut into slices
1/2 cup unfiltered apple juice

1 Place the banana slices in a plastic bag, close tightly, and freeze overnight or longer.

2 To make the "ice cream," place the bananas in a food processor. Start to run it, and pour the juice through the feed tube in a slow stream. Run for five or more minutes until the banana slices are completely pureed. Serve immediately. Makes 2 servings.

Peach Smoothie

1 cup orange juice or water
1 ripe peach, peeled and cut into chunks
1/2 banana, peeled

1 Process all in the blender until smooth. If too thick, add a bit more juice. Drink immediately. There are many variations of this drink, limited only by your imagination and the fresh fruits and juices available to you.

Teas

Among the better known herbs for calming and relaxing, we have camomile, catnip, and valerian. You can make a nice cup of tea with either of these, and sweeten to taste with a bit of honey or maple syrup.

The same herbs can also be added to a warm bath, with a similar effect. Valerian is particularly powerful. A note of caution, however: Don't have any of these if you're looking forward to a night of lovemaking with your partner!

As important as the food itself can be, the attitude you bring to eating it is just as important if not more. To be fully nourished, approach whatever you eat or drink with gratitude in your heart for the food and the life you've been given.

At The White House, A Taste of Virtue

Tongues are wagging throughout Epicuria. After all, Walter S. Scheib 3d, whom the White House has chosen as the new chef, has spent his career cooking in large hotels and health spas and is the only First Chef to speak enthusiastically about working with a physician to create low-fat dishes for the White House menu. Is this the first move toward establishing a diet-police state?

Historians say no: the decision is merely a response to the fact that dietary fat has become a demon in American culture. Like past administrations, this one is aware of the public attitude toward food and has chosen to take a stand that will reflect favorably on its character.

—*The New York Times*, April 6, 1994

ANNEMARIE COLBIN, CHES

CHAPTER 4

Aromatherapy

Roberta Wilson

Roberta Wilson is a licensed esthetician, a certified aromatherapist and a professional makeup artist. As a writer specializing in topics related to health and beauty, she has contributed over 150 articles to two dozen magazines. Her book, *Aromatherapy for Vibrant Health and Beauty* (Avery Publishing), is a comprehensive guide to aromatherapy treatments for health, skin and hair; Wilson also consults with natural cosmetic companies to develop aromatherapy cosmetics and public-relations programs.

*B*reathe in a beautiful bouquet of blossoms - chamomile, jasmine, lavender, rose and ylang ylang. As their sweet essence permeates the atmosphere and wafts up your nose, it slowly delivers you from the distresses of a demanding day at your desk to the serene sanctuary of a field of fragrant flowers freshly bathed by the morning dew. The delightful aromas enchant, almost intoxicate you. This is aromatherapy at its best—calming and relaxing you and reducing and soothing your stress.

Aromatherapy seduces your sense of smell with alluring aromatic essences, or essential oils. Within minutes, essential oils can transport you far from everyday worries and concerns into the realm of relaxation where you can begin to restore some semblance of sanity to your life. In the midst of modern times, aromatherapy can revive and rehabilitate your tired aching body and refresh and rejuvenate your weary mind, all of which help head you down the road toward greater relaxation and tranquility.

Since stress seems to be here to stay, it makes perfect sense to take advantage of aromatherapy's calming, relaxing and stress-reducing actions. Aromatherapy allows you to create your choice of moods and surround yourself with sensuous scents that increase your pleasure and enhance your enjoyment of life as they relax your body and mind.

WHAT IS AROMATHERAPY?

Throughout history, civilizations have relied on the natural healing and therapeutic properties of plants.

Aromatherapy is the ancient art of using concentrated essences ~ or essential oils ~ of certain aromatic plants to promote, enhance or restore physical, mental and emotional health and well-being. Essential oils are volatile oils that evaporate readily when exposed to air. They are usually very liquid and aren't greasy like canola, olive or sunflower oil.

Essential oils are extracted, usually by steam distillation, from the barks, leaves, petals, resins, rinds, roots, seeds, stalks or stems of certain aromatic plants, flowers, herbs or trees. They give plants their characteristic smell. Plants that contain essential oils store them in tiny pockets between their cell walls. Essential oils circulate throughout the plant delivering messages that assist the plant in performing functions such as metabolism, photosynthesis and cellular respiration. Some help plants adapt to environmental changes. They may repel insects and diseases or attract insects or animals to aid in pollination and propagation.

AROMATHERAPY'S LONG HISTORY

Throughout history, civilizations have relied on the natural healing and therapeutic properties of plants. Early records indicate that ancient Egyptians employed essential oils such as benzoin, cedarwood, frankincense, juniper, myrrh, rose and sandalwood for perfuming their skin, beautifying their bodies, aiding their meditations and maintaining physical and emotional health. They also used aromatic oils in religious rituals and in embalming.

Other ancient cultures used aromatic botanicals in their daily lives. Indians blended botanical oils such as jasmine, myrrh, sandalwood and rose for beauty, perfumery and sensual purposes as well as for assisting their spiritual development. Greeks greatly respected the healing powers of plants. They anointed each part of their bodies with different aromatic oils to contribute to their physical and emotional health. Romans enjoyed aromatics for bathing, cosmetics, hygiene, massage and medical treatments and the use of aromatherapy spread throughout the Roman empire.

Until the advent of modern science, botanicals remained the main source of most medicines, cosmetics and folk remedies.

Aromatherapy and the Ancients

In a sense, the origin of aromatherapy can be traced back to the origins of humanity, Some anthropologists believe that the appearance of some form of rituals is the defining moment of the emergence of human culture. Ever since the origins, rituals have always involved fumigations, the burning of aromatic herbs and woods. Rituals were used mostly in healing ceremonies. What a great intuition: by burning aromatic substances, fumigations diffuse essential oils into the air that have an antiseptic effect, bringing about physical healing. At the same time, the fragrance acts on a subtle level for psychic and spiritual healing.

—Marcel Lavabre, Founder, CEO, Aroma Vera

After the discovery of distillation by a tenth-century Arab physician, essential oils were easier to obtain and their use in perfumes became more prevalent, especially throughout Europe. During the sixteenth, seventeenth and eighteenth centuries some religious groups discouraged the use of essential oils and perfumes, claiming that they were too sensual, they were evil and even that they gave women an unfair advantage for seducing men. Despite this disapproval, their popularity continued.

Until the advent of modern science, botanicals remained the main source of most medicines, cosmetics and folk remedies. About one hundred years ago, scientists began synthesizing scents that smelled remarkably similar to nature's own creations. Even though these low-cost, readily-available laboratory alternatives lacked the therapeutic properties of essential oils, they slowly started to replace essential oils in cosmetics and medicines. Society became mesmerized by modern man-made products and almost forgot the natural health and beauty benefits of aromatherapy.

Eventually, people realized that these synthetic substitutes were not without problems. Synthetic fragrances frequently cause skin irritation and allergies. They are usually derived from petroleum, a non-renewable resource. Their price tag does not reflect their total cost to you and to the environment. In addition, a growing desire to return to a more natural lifestyle, a trend toward preventative health care and a willingness to assume responsibility for physical and emotional health also account for aromatherapy's recent revival and unprecedented popularity.

HOW ESSENTIAL OILS CAN AFFECT YOU

Essential oils most likely will affect your sense of smell first. As you open a bottle of an essential oil, its volatile aroma will diffuse throughout the environment. Odor molecules enter your nostrils and drift upward to your olfactory organ, where smell originates. There, hairlike cilia wave back and forth atop about ten million olfactory receptors located in the mucous membranes at the top of each nostril. These cilia detect scents and act as "keys," each one fitting a particular aroma that it "unlocks" or identifies.

Nearby nerves relay this odor information to the limbic region of the brain, where it can trigger memories and influence physical and emotional behavior. Smells can also stimulate the production of hormones and affect appetite, body temperature, hormone levels, insulin production, metabolism, stress levels and sex drive as well as immunity and conscious thoughts and reactions. The limbic system also affects the nervous system; desires, motivation, moods, intuition and creativity originate here. Besides enhancing your physical health, smells can make you feel better psychologically. Smells initiate both physiological and psychological responses by stimulating the release of neurotransmitters and endorphins in your brain. These hormone-like chemicals produce gratifying sensations, feelings of euphoria and generate an overall sense of well-being. Neurotransmitters can arouse sexual feelings, reduce stress, relieve pain and restore emotional equilibrium.

As you inhale essential oils, they enter your respiratory system as well. Inside your lungs, essential oils' minute molecules attach to oxygen molecules and travel into your blood stream, where they circulate throughout your body. Within individual cells, essential oils can activate your body's own abilities to help heal itself.

Because of the minute size of essential oils' molecules and your skin's porous nature, your skin can readily absorb them when they are applied topically. Once beneath the surface of your skin, essential oils wander through the intercellular fluid that surrounds your skin cells. From here, they enter your blood stream and can travel to your internal organs, lymph system and your immune system.

AROMATHERAPY'S POPULARITY

Aromatherapy has become one of the hottest buzz words of the nineties. Cosmetic companies and skin and hair care salons across the nation are capitalizing on essential oils' natural abilities to enhance the appearance of the skin, hair and body and to relieve some of the effects of stress that detract from beauty and well-being. From moisturizers to masks, from bath oils to body lotions, from shampoos to skin scrubs, from fragrances to facial oils, from creams to candles, aromatherapy products are lining the shelves of health food stores, body boutiques, department stores and drug stores.

Essential oils also play a principle role in the medical practices of many modern physicians. In Europe many doctors successfully prescribe essential oils and plant extracts instead of prescription drugs to treat their patients' physical problems or as a preventative measure to maintain their good health. In fact, the governments and insurance carriers in most European countries accept medical aromatherapy as a practical alternative to mainstream medicine. In this country, many naturopathic doctors realize the therapeutic value of aromatherapy and are using essential oils in their medical treatments.

European psychotherapists commonly recommend essential oils for the care of their patients. Some mental health clinics and hospitals even disperse essential oils into the atmosphere to calm, comfort and relax patients. Some American psychotherapists use aromatherapy to accelerate results. Many massage therapists see the remarkable relaxing and stress-reducing actions that aromatherapy has on their clients. All across America and abroad people are discovering the difference that aromatherapy can make in their lives.

How Aromatherapy Can Enrich Your Life

Aromatherapy gently and naturally activates your body's own healing energies to restore balance to your body, mind and emotions. Besides calming your frazzled nerves and relaxing your tension-filled muscles, aromatherapy can enhance the quality of your life by improving your health, prompting your body and mind to function more efficiently, boosting your immune system and heightening your sensory awareness.

One of aromatherapy's biggest benefits is reducing and managing stress. Stress is an unavoidable side effect of modern life and plays a primary role in almost all illnesses, both physical and mental. Successful stress management relaxes you and takes your mind off your sources of stress. Aromatherapy can do just that.

Aromatherapy can quiet the commotion and confusion in your mind and distract you from the drudgery of your day, giving you a chance to catch your breath and alter your attitude. You can then return to your daily duties feeling revitalized, rejuvenated and more capable of conquering the tasks at hand.

Essential oils can elevate your moods, soothe your emotions and clear your mind. Many can help you regulate your moods. Some are uplifting and energizing while others are calming and sedating. Several return your body and mind to a more balanced state.

Aromatherapy is also one of the most natural and effective approaches to personal care for both men and women. Aromatherapy skin and body treatments can add a new dimension to your beauty routine and improve the appearance of your skin. Essential oils can revitalize dry or prematurely aging skin, regulate oily skin, clear problem skin and add a healthy glow to all complexions. Essential oils such as bergamot, chamomile, jasmine, lavender, marjoram, neroli, rose and ylang ylang relax you, while basil, benzoin, black pepper, eucalyptus, geranium, juniper, lemon, peppermint and rosemary oils recharge, revitalize and stimulate you. In addition, clary sage, coriander, elemi, fennel, frankincense, palmarosa, rosewood, sandalwood and vetiver also help lower stress levels. Oils such as basil, benzoin, cedarwood, geranium, lavender, lemon, myrrh, orange, patchouli and thyme help balance you - either stimulating or relaxing you, depending on your body's needs. Aromatherapy complements almost any other type of therapy or treatments, either conventional or alternative.

Regular use of aromatherapy can make a big difference in the way you look, feel and smell and it can also help you cope with life's many challenges. Because aromatherapy gently encourages you to relax and slow down, you tend to take better care of yourself. When you treat yourself well, you feel better about yourself and your life. Stress subsides. Tension melts. Peace, happiness and joy can become a more permanent part of your life. You generally gain a greater appreciation of life and all its many privileges and blessings. Once you're relaxed and refreshed, you can more readily reach your full potential in any realm you pursue.

WAYS TO INTRODUCE AROMATHERAPY INTO YOUR LIFE

You can easily introduce aromatherapy into your daily life in an assortment of ways: baths, skin and body care, environmental fragrancing, personal perfumes and fragrances, inhalants and massage. The following descriptions will help you determine which methods will best suit you and your lifestyle. Once you start using aromatherapy and realize the difference it makes, you'll wonder how you ever managed without it.

Time Out Baths

As you submerge yourself in an aromatherapy bath, you can surrender your tension-filled body and your emotionally-exhausted mind to the relaxation that awaits you. As you soak, let revitalizing and rejuvenating essential oils soothe sore muscles as they smooth and soften your skin.

Bathing regularly with essential oils helps control stress, alleviate anxiety, ease tension and minimize muscular aches and pains. Aromatherapy can turn the daily act of cleansing your body into a relaxing ritual. You'll emerge feeling refreshed and ready to conquer your chores, dive into your deadlines or just sink into your sheets and sleep soundly like a baby.

 **DIRECTIONS** Add a total of six to ten drops of essential oils to a tub of water. Soak ten to twenty minutes. Or use one of the Time Out Bath Blends following. To increase your enjoyment, before plunging into the tub, turn off the telephone, play some soft music, light a candle and add *Stress-Relieving Diffuser* blend to the diffuser.

Time Out Bath Blends		
Nighttime Relaxation Bath	**Stress-Reduction Bath**	**Muscle-Relief Bath Blend**
4 drops lavender oil 3 drops chamomile oil 2 drops marjoram oil 2 drops ylang ylang oil	3 drops lavender oil 2 drops coriander oil 2 drops geranium oil 2 drops orange oil	4 drops chamomile oil 3 drops bergamot oil 2 drops clary sage oil 2 drops coriander oil
Add to a tub of warm water. Soak for 20 to 30 minutes.	Add to a tub of warm water. Soak for 20 to 30 minutes.	Add to a tub of warm water. Soak for 20 to 30 minutes.

Skin and Body Care

Personal care is one of the most popular application for aromatherapy. Besides preserving youthfulness and an attractive appearance, taking care of your skin and body helps subdue stress. Many essential oils can improve circulation to the skin and stimulate cell renewal while they calm your emotions.

You can choose commercial aromatherapy products, you can customize unscented commercial products by adding essential oils or you can make your own aromatherapy cosmetics. See the chart *Relaxing and Rejuvenating Essential Oils for Your Skin* to decide which oils will work best for you.

DIRECTIONS To customize unscented products, as a general rule, add eight to ten drops of an essential oil or an essential oil blend to one ounce of the product. Mix well and use according to directions.

You can also make your own aromatherapy facial oils and body oils by adding five to ten drops of an essential oil or an essential oil blend to one ounce of an unscented carrier oil such as jojoba, canola oil or sunflower oil.

CAUTION: Always dilute essential oils before applying them to your skin.

Revitalizing & Refreshing Facial Oil

1/2 ounce jojoba oil
4 drops lavender oil
3 drops sandalwood oil
2 drops geranium oil

Combine. Apply several drops to clean skin. Follow with *Soothing Facial Spray.*

Soothing Facial Spray

8 ounces distilled water
3 drops lavender oil
2 drops chamomile oil
1 drop ylang ylang oil

Add oils to water. Spray your face frequently. Shake well before each use.

Skin-Softening Splash

8 ounce distilled water
5 drops lavender oil
2 drops rosewood oil
1 drop neroli oil

Combine. Splash on your skin after cleansing.

Stress-Soothing Skin Softening Oil

4 ounces canola or sunflower oil
10 drops lavender oil
8 drops chamomile oil
6 drops clary sage oil
6 drops geranium oil
4 drops ylang ylang oil
3 drops benzoin resin

Combine. Smooth over skin after bathing or showering.

Nerve-Nourishing Facial Mask

1 tbsp. French green clay
1 tsp. honey
1 drop clary sage oil
1 drop lavender oil
1 drop ylang ylang oil

Combine ingredients in your palm. Add water, if necessary, to form a paste. Apply to face and neck. Lie down and relax for 10 to 15 minutes. Rinse with warm water. Apply *Skin Softening Splash*, then *Revitalizing & Refreshing Facial Oil*.

Fragrancing Your Environment

Aromatherapy diffusers and lamps can quickly fragrance your environment as they create various moods. They disperse minute molecules of essential oils throughout your room, home or office as well as purify, cleanse and remove unpleasant odors. Diffusers are electrically-powered air pumps that can fragrance a room or an entire home. Lamps have small bowls that hold water and essential oils and a candle or a little light bulb generates heat that releases the aroma of the essential oils. Create your own diffuser blends by combining three or four of your favorite stress-reducing scents in a glass bottle. Or use one of the formulas on the next page.

DIRECTIONS With most diffusers, you simply attach a bottle of essential oil, plug in the diffuser and turn it on. Follow the directions for your diffuser. For lamps, fill the small bowl with water and add five to twenty drops of essential oils. Turn on the heat source ~ either a candle or an electric light bulb ~ and enjoy the aromas that waft into the atmosphere.

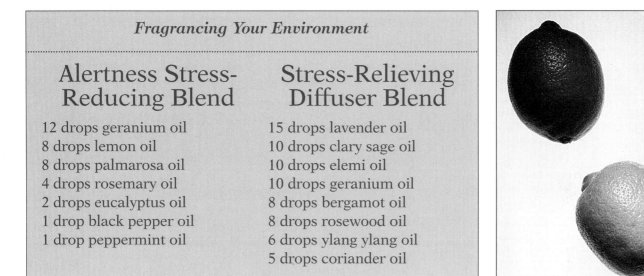

Fragrancing Your Environment

Alertness Stress-Reducing Blend

12 drops geranium oil
8 drops lemon oil
8 drops palmarosa oil
4 drops rosemary oil
2 drops eucalyptus oil
1 drop black pepper oil
1 drop peppermint oil

Stress-Relieving Diffuser Blend

15 drops lavender oil
10 drops clary sage oil
10 drops elemi oil
10 drops geranium oil
8 drops bergamot oil
8 drops rosewood oil
6 drops ylang ylang oil
5 drops coriander oil

Fragrances and Perfumes

Creating your own perfumes with essential oils offers a pleasing, natural alternative to commercial fragrances, which are made almost exclusively of synthetic petrochemicals. Besides their lovely aroma, natural fragrances can be quite therapeutic both emotionally and physically, whereas synthetic scents are often offensive and can cause allergies and sensitivities. When you feel stressed out or simply need to slow down and relax, dab a few drop on your pulse points, your temples, the back of your neck and on the tip of your nose. Breathe in the natural aroma and relax.

DIRECTIONS As a general guideline, add ten to twenty drops of essential oils to 1/8 ounce of jojoba oil. Jojoba oil is the best carrier oil for fragrances; it doesn't go rancid and won't spoil your perfume. You can make your fragrances as intense or subtle as you desire by your choice of essential oils and the amount of each oil you use. To prevent skin irritation, don't apply pure essential oils directly to your skin. See blends in column on the next page.

Fine Flower Fragrance for Women

1/8 ounce jojoba oil
8 drops rose oil
8 drops neroli oil
4 drops jasmine oil
2 drops geranium oil
2 drops ylang ylang oil

Combine in a small glass bottle. Apply as perfume.

Stress-Reducing Scent for Men

1/8 ounce jojoba oil
12 drops sandalwood oil
4 drops clary sage oil
2 drops coriander oil
2 drops vetiver oil
1 drop benzoin resin
1 drop ylang ylang oil

Mix together in a small glass bottle. Apply as a fragrance.

Stress-Reducing Inhalant

Relaxing Breathing Blend

10 drops lavender oil
8 drops bergamot oil
6 drops ylang ylang oil
4 drops chamomile oil
4 drops clary sage oil
2 drops benzoin resin

Blend in a small glass bottle Whiff whenever needed.

Inhalants

For quick relief from anxiety, emotional upsets and stress or simply to encourage relaxation, inhale an essential oil directly from the bottle. You can choose a single oil, create your own combination or use the blend in column on the right.

DIRECTIONS Blend your choice of essential oils in a small glass bottle. Open the bottle and inhale the aroma. You can also add two or three drops of the blend to a tissue or handkerchief and inhale it that way. Carry your inhalant with you for a refreshing aromatherapy break almost anywhere.

Massage

Incorporating essential oils into massage is a marvelous way to promote relaxation, minimize muscular aches and pain, subdue stress and tension and treat a variety of conditions in a pleasant, relaxing way. Besides feeling great, massage can soothe your nervous system, reduce blood pressure, relax your muscles, diminish swelling and stimulate blood and lymph flow. It also can release cellular wastes from your muscles, relax your breathing and slow your pulse.

If you receive professional massages, ask your massage therapist to use your aromatherapy massage oil blends. Self-massage works well, too. Whether you massage deep into your own muscles or lightly spread massage oil onto your skin, you will derive great benefits.

DIRECTIONS Make your own massage and skin oils by adding ten drops of an essential oil or essential oil blend to one ounce of carrier oil. Blend well. Apply over your body with either long sweeping strokes or short overlapping strokes. You can knead an area or make circular movements. You can also tap an area with your fingertips. See blends below.

Massage from your feet upward toward your heart. From your fingers stroke toward your heart. Massage your abdomen in a clockwise direction from your right side to the left along your large intestines. Begin on your lower right abdomen and stroke upward and across your abdomen above your navel. Continue downward along the left side of your abdomen.

Massage Oils

Relaxation Massage Oil

2 ounces carrier oil
10 drops chamomile oil
8 drops marjoram oil
4 drops ylang ylang oil
3 drops benzoin resin

Blend ingredients. Massage onto skin daily.

Stress-Soothing Massage Oil

2 ounces carrier oil
8 drops sandalwood oil
6 drops lavender oil
4 drops chamomile oil
3 drops bergamot oil
3 drops marjoram oil
2 drops elemi oil

Blend. ingredients. Massage onto skin daily.

ESSENTIAL OILS THAT ENCOURAGE RELAXATION & REDUCE STRESS

BASIL   Basil oil increases concentration, sharpens the senses, clarifies thoughts and calms nervousness. It can either sedate or stimulate. Its sedative qualities ward off anxiety attacks and nervous tension and help relieve insomnia. Its stimulating action fights mental fatigue and strengthens mental functions.

BENZOIN   Benzoin has a warming and soothing effect on emotions. It calms and pacifies the mind, eases nervous tension, stress and anxiety and soothes frazzled nerves. Its uplifting effect helps decrease depression and restore confidence.

BERGAMOT   Bergamot oil is a refreshing, uplifting oil that acts as a stimulant to balance emotions and moods. It can relieve anxiety, diminish depression and calm anger.

BLACK PEPPER   Black pepper oil increases alertness and improves concentration. It stimulates mental energy, especially blocked energy. It is a very settling oil that provides a sense of protection.

CEDARWOOD   Cedarwood oil eases anxiety, nervous tension and stress-related conditions. It also calms emotions and restores energy imbalances. Cedarwood oil helps maintain emotional composure.

CHAMOMILE   Chamomile oil is a calming and relaxing oil and most people prefer its subtle sedative action to harsh, habit-forming prescription tranquilizers. It helps create emotional stability and helps combat anxiety, stress, depression, nervousness and insomnia.

CLARY SAGE   Clary sage oil helps restore inner tranquility and minimizes the debilitating effects of stress. It calms and relaxes your body and mind. It reduces muscular aches and pains and restores emotional equilibrium.

CORIANDER   Coriander oil refreshes and energizes as it relaxes and calms anxiety, stress or nervousness. It relieves mental fatigue and nervousness and improves memory functions and creativity.

ELEMI   Elemi oil revitalizes and relaxes minds overwhelmed with stress and mental or emotional exhaustion. It calms nervousness and promotes peacefulness and clarity. It also aids meditation.

Coriander

EUCALYPTUS   Eucalyptus oil can restore balance during times of emotional overload. It is stimulating and refreshing and can help overcome sluggishness. It also increases concentration.

FENNEL   Fennel oil calms emotions, reduces stress and eases nervousness. It provides a sense of protection and support during emotionally vulnerable times.

FRANKINCENSE   Frankincense oil revitalizes the body and mind after bouts of mental or physical exhaustion. It soothes mental anxiety, nervous tension or stress and is comforting to the emotions. By slowing respiration, frankincense oil produces a sense of serenity and can calm restlessness.

GERANIUM   Geranium oil soothes away stress, anxiety and tension and helps restore emotional equilibrium. Some people respond to geranium oil's sedative, somewhat analgesic effect, while others claim it stimulates them. Most people find it simultaneously calming and energizing.

Eucalyptus

JASMINE   Jasmine diminishes anxiety, depression, nervous exhaustion and stress. It helps relax the mind, balance moods and elevate the spirits. Jasmine inspires a greater appreciation of the beauty in the world.

JUNIPER   Juniper helps overcome anxiety, nervous tension and stress-related conditions. It can clear mental confusion, revive exhausted emotions and strengthen the nerves. Juniper imparts a feeling of emotional cleanliness and purity.

LAVENDER   Lavender oil balances extremes of emotions and contributes to emotional equilibrium by reducing stress. It relaxes the mind and promotes physical and mental well-being. It helps neutralize sensory overload and balance either a racing or sluggish mind. At bedtime it can help overcome insomnia.

General Guidelines for Using Essential Oils

• Use only pure essential oils, never substitute synthetics.

• Buy from reliable sources that guarantee the purity of their oils.

• Dilute essential oils in a carrier oil such as almond, apricot kernel, canola, hazelnut, jojoba or sunflower oil. Essential oils are highly concentrated and even one drop of pure essential oil, applied directly to your skin, can cause an irritation.

Essential oils are extremely concentrated; sometimes they are 100 times stronger than the fresh plant or dried herb.

• Trust your nose. If you dislike the smell of a certain oil, don't use it.

• Inhale essential oils for short periods only. Run your diffuser for about five to ten minutes at a time.

• Follow the directions for the aromatherapy blends. Never add more than the recommended number of drops, although you can use fewer drops if you wish.

• If you have doubts about using an essential oil or an aromatherapy blend, trust your instincts or check with a qualified aromatherapist or your health-care professional.

• When using essential oils on infants or children, dilute one to three drops of essential oils in one ounce of carrier oil. Use two to six drops of the diluted oil in a bath. For inhalations add one drop of essential oil to the bowl of water.

• If you experience any irritation, sensitization or unpleasant reaction, discontinue use.

• Never take essential oils internally unless you are under the supervision of a health-care professional trained in practice of medical aromatherapy.

Note: If you have any serious physical ailments or if you have any concerns or doubts about using essential oils, please consult your health care professional before using any of the essential oils or aromatherapy blends suggested in this book.

LEMON   Lemon is refreshing and uplifting for the emotions. It fights stress. It can calm or prevent emotional outbursts. It also improves concentration and stimulates the memory.

MARJORAM   Marjoram oil calms emotions and minimizes emotional upsets, making it useful for anxiety attacks, emotional exhaustion, nervous tension, and stress-related problems. It relaxes both the mind and the muscles. At nighttime it can help overcome insomnia.

MYRRH   Myrrh is cooling and calming for the emotions. It stimulates the mind and improves clarity and focus. It provides strength to endure challenging times.

NEROLI   Neroli oil calms and soothes emotions and subdues stress. It acts as a natural tranquilizer, dispersing anger and nervousness and imparting a sense of joy and peace. It provides support to continue during mental or psychological exhaustion.

ORANGE   Orange oil calms and relaxes nerves and helps combat anxiety, stress and insomnia. It revitalizes emotional energy and balances emotions, either relaxing or stimulating as needed.

PALMAROSA   Palmarosa oil reduces stress and tension. It calms and uplifts the emotions while refreshing the mind and clarifying thoughts. It helps stimulate recovery from nervous exhaustion.

PATCHOULI   Patchouli oil eases anxiety, nervous exhaustion and stress-related conditions. It reduces mental fatigue and calms emotional upset. In low doses it is sedating, while it is stimulating in larger quantities.

PEPPERMINT   Peppermint oil helps calm nervousness and relieve mental fatigue. It eases anxiety and fights depression. Peppermint increases alertness, improves concentration and clears thought processes.

ROSE   Rose oil soothes the emotions, lifts the spirits and reduces stress and tension. It helps calm nerves, alleviate anxiety and diminish depression. It stabilizes mood swings and helps balance emotions. It helps overcome insomnia.

ROSEMARY   Rosemary oil relaxes nerves, balances intense emotions and regulates mood swings. It lifts spirits, reduces mental strain and assists in overcoming stress-related disorders. Rosemary oil fights mental fatigue and sluggishness by arousing energy.

ROSEWOOD   Rosewood calms and relaxes and helps relieve anxiety, tension and stress. It balances emotions and steadies nerves. It is uplifting, especially in stressful situations and for fatigue.

SANDALWOOD   Sandalwood soothes emotional exhaustion and soothes stress. It relaxes the body and mind and elevates the spirits, helping to release tension, nervousness and stress. Sandalwood stimulates the senses and clears thought processes.

THYME   Thyme eases nervousness and stress. It helps balance you, either keeping you alert or helping you to sleep. It can stimulate the mind during mental or emotional fatigue, increase concentration and enhance memory.

VETIVER   Vetiver oil helps balance the nervous system and is emotionally calming and regenerative. It alleviates anxiety, stress and tension and helps settles the nerves. It can restore balance and harmony to your life.

YLANG YLANG   Ylang ylang relaxes and calms excited emotional states and promotes positive emotions. It subdues stress, eases anxiety and stabilizes moods. It fosters feelings of love, security and peacefulness. It activates enthusiasm and provides comfort during times of transition.

Relaxing and Rejuvenating Essential Oils for Your Skin

NORMAL	DRY	OILY	MATURE	SENSITIVE
clary sage	benzoin	clary sage	benzoin	chamomile
elemi	bergamot	elemi	clary sage	frankincense
frankincense	clary sage	frankincense	elemi	jasmine
geranium	elemi	geranium	fennel	neroli
jasmine	fennel	jasmine	frankincense	rose
lavender	frankincense	neroli	geranium	rosewood
neroli	geranium	orange	jasmine	sandalwood
palmarosa	jasmine	palmarosa	neroli	
rose	lavender	rosemary	palmarosa	
rosemary	neroli	rosewood	rose	
rosewood	palmarosa	sandalwood	rosemary	
sandalwood	rose	vetiver	sandalwood	
vetiver	rosemary	ylang ylang	vetiver	
	rosewood			
	sandalwood			
	vetiver			

CHAPTER 5

Breath & Voice

Don G. Campbell

Don G. Campbell is Director of the Institute for Music, Health and Education and the Therapeutic Sound School in Boulder, Colorado, Minneapolis, San Francisco and Philadelphia. He is author of seven books, including: *Music, Physician for Times to Come, Music and Miracles, The Roar of Silence* and *Introduction to the Musical Brain.* He has released seven albums of music composed for the body from the body as well as written two ballets including "Dances for a Sleepwalker." A classical musician, he studied with Nadia Boulanger in France, served as a music critic in Japan, and has worked with the Guggenheim project in contemporary education in Chicago.

The body is equipped with many natural accessories for the release of stress, tension and pain. Yet it has only been in the past few decades that recognition of the natural use of the voice for refreshment, health maintenance and curation has been developed. The power of the word, poetics, and song as well as the emotional cries of joy, pain and sorrow are only a small part of the voice's ability to express, release and charge the mind and body.

Exercise, a balanced diet, meditation, as well as a variety of massage techniques have begun to integrate medicine with expressive therapies and well-being programs. Yet, the most innate and natural way to release stress, relax or bring gratification to the mind, emotions and body ~ via the sounds we can produce ~ is completely self-generated.

HEALING SOUND

Every vowel at every pitch in a variety of postures creates dynamic uses of the voice as a healing instrument.

The most innovative healing work with sound is concerned with the "energy inside of sound." Rather than being concerned with the acoustic aspects of what we hear, there is an awareness of the energy within sound waves that moves liquids, solids, as well as molecules in the air. Living organs respond to sounds in a variety of ways. Twenty years ago, Dorothy Rentallack's experimented with plants and the music of Bach, Ravi Shankar and Led Zeppelin (and her work has been basic to later experiments.) She realized that Indian Raga music and Baroque music cause plants to bloom more quickly and healthfully. Within the past few years French acupuncturist and musician researcher Fabien Mammon has explored the nature of tone, elongated vowel sounds, on cancer cells as well as healthy cells. Prolonged tones create altogether different reactions from the cells, and in laboratory experiments have actually destroyed cancer cells. Presently, experiments are being done to understand molecular response to rhythmic and melodic patterning.

At the Institute for Music, Health and Education in Boulder, Colorado, I have led six years of exploration into self-generated tones through the voice. By developing a daily routine of elongated vowel sounds, each student has developed an emotional, physical and mental glossary of the effects of self-generated sounds. Every vowel at every pitch in a variety of postures creates dynamic uses of the voice as a healing instrument. Every individual is unique and has a variety of responses to the tension and relaxation expressed through the voice.

Most of the experiments have been done through correspondence courses that utilize journals, tapes and intuitive circular drawings to record emotions and physical tensions.

How I came to study and teach these techniques is a story in itself. Being a classically trained musician, I became aware of stress at an early age with recitals, contests and the constant pressure of performing well at every lesson. At age thirteen I was accepted in the Fontainebleau Conservatory of Music under the direction of Nadia Boulanger. Soon I became aware that my classmates were college professors, professional composers and performers as well as graduate students from colleges all over the world. They all worried about concerts, about being called on in class, and about the private lessons where Mademoiselle Boulanger would examine their creative works.

By the time I was in graduate school studying conducting, I was aware that stress was an essential part of the music mastery process: "No pain, no gain, thus no competitive mastery of musical art." Each semester we would perform in front of a "jury." I always knew I was *innocent* when I entered the musical world with a child-like mind. Later I was *guilty* of buying into the stress, guilt and exhaustion of becoming a classical musician.

It was not until my mid-thirties that I realized that this conscious competition had created a constant unconscious stress within me. The beginnings of a degenerative bone disease as well as a lump in my lungs gave me a full indication that I was also losing the joy of sound, music and my voice. As a child I was relaxed, spontaneous and filled with the constant, natural power of sound. Naturally, I was drawn to a life in music. Before all the training in music, I had truly been in love with sound. Yet by mid-life, I had slowly sacrificed and given away the essence of my own connection with the life force that music provided me.

New Year's Eve, 1981, as I was writing my resolutions and meditating on my life, a gradual hum, a growl came from my voice. I felt an unexpressed, natural sound begin to emerge from my emotions and body through my voice. What began as a few emotional minutes of stressful malcontent and melancholy, unfolded into hours and hours of emotional release through vocal soundings, movement and drumming. From the suburban neighborhood of north Dallas came the primal, essential voice. Neither beautiful, nor elegant, it overrode all my expressive education and jolted me into a heartfelt anguish through the wailing sounds of my voice.

For thirty-five hours I experienced an altered state of awareness where my voice, body and mind explored the power of my own forgotten tool for healing and relaxation. I realized that I had never allowed the emotions to be released through the natural sobs, whines, *ahs*, *ooous* and *ughs* that were easily available. My natural ways of release had been held so tightly bound within me that my own foundation and skeletal structure had begun to deteriorate. Once I had surrendered to the sounds, the extraordinary power and naturalness of my cry, whimper and grief, another type of sound began to emerge. It was a hum, a tone that vibrated my body from the inside out. "It" was a deeper part of myself that was able to balance and rejuvenate. It held the seeds of joy, balance and refreshment. It provided a place of relaxation, renewal and positive acceptance of all that was evident in my life.

For four years I spent about ten minutes each morning humming a sound that was neither musical nor beautiful before my meditation and contemplative practice. I noticed how relaxed and simple meditation became.

Each day there was an intuitive place that I could find in my voice that would release stress, bring a sense of centering and peace to both my mind and body. I was amazed that meditation became easy and that my body was strong and at ease. There were no longer any signs of the bone degeneration nor the lump in my left lung. Healing had occurred.

I then began to experiment with vowel sounds, twice a day in a variety of postures. I noticed that each time I used these self-generated sounds there was a modification of my awareness. Each day the experience was different and unique. I found the *eee* sound to be stimulating and activating most of the time. Yet, on occasion it was piercing, disturbing and out of alignment with what I felt to be my emotional needs. Sometimes the sound would work like caffeine and other times it would release a tremendous amount of tension. *Eee* had a wide variety of

I have discovered that every person holds a map of consciousness within the voice.

qualities. I stayed on the same pitch for each of the sessions. My voice would find a comfortable, unstrained tone. I would let it rest there, moving up and down only to accommodate a natural ease.

Often I had the urge to chant or sing. I would notice that the tone tempted me to improve and create songs. I found that by not moving around the pitch with tunes or overtones, a sensitivity to a power within the sound itself became more apparent, though it was less musical.

THE VOICE AND CONSCIOUSNESS

In a decade of exploration of the vowel sounds with over a thousand students, I have discovered that every person holds a map of consciousness within the voice. The energy inside the voice directly affects the mind and body. Nothing is more efficient and natural than the voice as a instrument to massage the bones, organs and skin from the inside out. It is a natural accessory for the release of tension, the stimulation of the mind, the expression of thoughts and bridging the emotions with the mind.

Self-generated sounds and images may soon lead the field in the healing arts. What was standard practice in the most ancient forms of Eastern and shamanic healing practices is gradually gaining attention in the medical community. Forms of drumming, singing, and chanting all create endorphin releases that reduce pain, calm the mind, lower brain wave patterns and balance the body. Music therapists are using the voice as a tool for healing the link between conscious expression and physical disabilities.

New forms of healing and relaxation modalities insist that the generation of the vibration comes from within the client rather than through the instrument, the drum, a recording or the voice or music of the therapist. New systems of healing are truly "Do it yourself." "Tune in and tune up."

This may sound overly simplistic, but self-created relaxation is actually a repatterning and retraining of the mind and body through various levels of sound production from the voice and muscle rhythms of the body. Anyone who has had physical therapy for a broken bone or a severely strained mus-

Self-generated sounds and images may soon lead the field in the healing arts.

Landmark Research in the

The most important researcher in discovering the voice's function and ability in regard to health and well-being is Alfred A. Tomatis, M.D. For decades he worked as an ear and throat specialist. His father, a famous French opera singer, compelled Dr. Tomatis to explore the voice's problems. When he would treat singers he realized that the volume and power of their own voices sometimes harmed their own physical abilities to relax and stay healthy. Stress in the voice modified their listening and tuning abilities. He even found that a singer could create near deafness by singing improperly.

Dr. Tomatis' hearing assessments with workers in airline factories during the Second World War provided the important data that led him to believe and prove that the sounds the voice makes are directly associated to the ability of the ear to hear, listen and discriminate sound.

There are psychological elements that drastically determine how the ear focuses on outer information and how the voice reveals inner information about emotions, health and mentality. Dr. Tomatis found that the voice can actually alter the physiological and neurological ability to receive sound. By testing the air

cle knows that the therapist can only provide attentiveness and technique to regain the healthy pattern. We actually orchestrate our own healing.

When vocal sounds are blended with suggestions or images, the physical response is greatest. Whether it is a style of guided imagery or free-flowing associations, the mind-body connections are made more easily available with the use of music.

Relaxing is an important key to survival in our challenging, stressful world where we no longer live as essentially in the natural rhythms of the seasons. Learning to orchestrate relaxation can be a challenge. It is sometimes hard to find the time to meditate, do yoga or even walk the dog. With the voice and the awareness of making inner sounds in the mind, you can begin to find effective and readily available ways to tune in and tune up your consciousness, body and emotions.

Voice-Ear Connection

and bone conduction curves in each ear, He was able to prove that the physical state of the body, the psychological history and the emotional states of the mind are reflected in the vocal and auditory assessment.

Dr. Tomatis has researched the relationship of the voice with the ear and found that "The Voice Can Only Produce What the Ear Can Hear." This theory has been recognized by the French Academy of Sciences through Dr. Tomatis' listening assessments. By stimulating and exercising certain frequency bands through specific filters and gates, the Tomatis Method often restores many levels of mental attentiveness and richness of voice that may have been lost or injured. Although his techniques and methods do not correct many kinds of deafness, it is almost miraculous in how it assists students with reading, writing and motor disabilities. Attention disorders, dyslexia and even forms of severe autism has been greatly improved with a special instrument called the Electronic Ear, developed to stimulate the voice-ear relationship. Dr. Tomatis' autobiography, *The Conscious Ear*, (Station Hill Press) is a fascinating story about the miracles in the vocal and auditory worlds.

The following exercises are designed for the novice as well as the expert in relaxation. Using the voice as a primary or secondary tool is the goal in the following exercises. Although they sound easy, obvious and quite unsophisticated, grant yourself two weeks to explore their power, their ease and remarkable results.

I Am Vibration

EXERCISE Sit comfortably in a chair so there is a feeling of relaxing upward. Close your eyes and imagine your whole body as a balloon. Upon inhalation, sense your body expanding with ease. With each exhalation, visualize your body releasing air from every pore in the body.

For two or three minutes continue to sense the balloon gently expanding and releasing with deep and long exhalations and inhalations.

When you feel comfortable with the breath, then relax the jaw and allow a HUM to begin. It is not a melody, a chant or a tune. It is a tone. This tone is not being made for the purpose of being beautiful or musical. It is being made for the purpose of massaging the body from the inside out. The jaw is loose, the teeth are slightly apart and the lips are together. The sound is low and soft. In your mind, think:

I am exhaling tension by massaging the body and mind
with vibration.
I am inhaling harmony and well-being.
I am vibration.

Four to five minutes of this exercise each morning and evening for a week will tune up your world. Let your critical, verbal brain take a rest and allow the rest of your brain and body to naturally attune itself.

Relax with Vowels

Each of us remembers being told to "be quiet", "hush", "be still" and "don't cry." The voice is an immediate indicator of our state of mind and body. It is a natural accessory to release pain and stress throughout our lives. When a child cries there is a release of stress and pain. The voice signals fear and emotional concern. Often we treat the voice and not the wound or emotional state.

It is disconcerting to hear crying and sobbing, yet it is the body's way to soothe itself, come to completion of an emotion and allow the fullness of grief, pain, sorrow or stress to be released. The release of energy with the voice is generally a private affair. There is such a vast amount of emotional and physical energy that can be released, the need for privacy to explore the power of simple sounds is important.

Do not be misled. These sounds do not have to be loud. Although there are times when the energy is charged and must be released, the relaxation that is brought to the body and mind is generally more effective in the gentle, quiet and soothing sounds.

EXERCISE Set aside a time where you can explore the vowel sounds. Sit comfortably in a chair and exhale a few times releasing thought. Then for three to five minutes begin to tone with a relaxed jaw. Place the palm of your hand just below your throat so that it rests comfortably on the upper part of your chest. Bring the other hand to your cheek and allow your head to gently rest on your hand. Close your eyes.

- Day One   Open the lips slightly and make an *eh* sound

- Day Two   Relax the jaw and make an *eee* sound

- Day Three Make a gentle *ah* sound

- Day Four   Make a long restful *oh* sound

- Day Five   Make a gentle *ouuu* sound

Imagine you are deaf and that all the energy of the sounds is massaging your body from within. Let your hands be your ears and sense the vibratory power. Do not look for an outcome, just be aware of the presence.

After your time of toning, put your hands in your lap, keep the eyes closed and deeply sense your body and mind. You may wish to record your impressions in a journal.

Each vowel at every pitch has a different power. Each person responds differently. I suggest that your voice be lower in pitch as you begin this tonal awareness. Keep the same pitch for most of the time you are toning. If ever you feel strain or stress, just stop for thirty seconds. Then renew the exercise. If you feel it is just time to stop, then just stop.

At times an emotion or a memory may arise. You can choose to tone right through that memory and allow it to be cleared away, or you may come to rest and know that you will work with that feeling at a later time. The wisdom of the vowels in the body is extraordinary. Become aware of their power to charge, relax and heal the body.

A Hard Day at the Office

Routines make us feel safe, give clarity and rhythm to our lives. Our daily patterns give us a sense of stability. If we plan a deviation to our working or living patterns as a vacation, we find refreshment, release and excitement. But when the car breaks down, or a snow storm keeps us from getting to work, or our health fails, tension becomes a companion.

Not all tension is negative. Learning how to orchestrate tension and release is a fundamental tool for health. Learning how to prevent tension, how to release it and relax during the daily routines is the magic of creative health.

If you drive alone to and from work, you have an ideal stress release chamber. There is no one to judge you, except that internal voice that may need a little time to trust the power of healing with your voice. Here are some easy vocal prescriptions that may assist you along each working day.

SONIC CAFFEINE   On your way to work, instead of a cup of coffee to charge your day and rev up the body's pace, replace it with twelve long exhalations. Add to your breath an *eh* sound. Keep the jaw relaxed and allow the *eh* sound to be natural, not forced, just bright. This sound will help you charge your day, reduce fatigue and grogginess. Use this technique when you wake up or in the car.

A RELAXED BREATH   We often think that by taking a deep breath we are relaxing. Actually the greatest relaxation response comes through concentrating on a deep exhalation. Just exhale a dozen times without any concentration on the incoming breath. Go to the bottom of your breath and then allow the incoming breath just to fill the body naturally with no effort. Notice how you feel. Add a humming sound to the released breath and you will likely begin to yawn.

During the work day, you may not be able to make sounds without disturbing others. So practice the exhalation with an internal sound *ah*. The suggestion of the sound is sometimes as powerful a tool as the actual sound. The internalized use of sound is advanced work, but some simple exploration of your own silent, internal thoughts of sound is most useful.

DON G. CAMPBELL

WHY IS RUSH HOUR SO SLOW? "I've been rushing all day, I think the only thing that rushes in rush hour is my brain." Traffic slows down because of congestion, but we call it rush hour! Actually, the reason rush hour causes stress is that we cannot relax or harmonize with the rhythm and pace of that time of day.

An outstanding exercise for the late afternoon car ride home is to make clear vocal sounds as to the nature of your day. Make up a new language and gibber it out loud to yourself. Let the emotions and the stories be retold and expressed but in words you are making up.

Try finding a sound that reflects your emotions. Empowering the body to release tensions through the voice is primary. "I just want to scream with the way my associate talks to me." The tension held from daily experiences goes deeply into the body and unconscious mind. So before sleep in the evening, tone for five to ten minutes to release the pressure of the day.

The morning exercises charge, clarify and center your day. The evening exercises release the tension and stress of the day so that sleep and rest are more available. Naturally the brighter vowel sounds *eh* and *eee* charge and activate the body. Whereas the *ah* and *oh* relax the body. Test all the vowels coming and going from the office and build you own sonic vocabulary.

Healing the Inner Listener

EXERCISE Sit comfortably with eyes closed, in a quiet place where your body can be supported gently. Spend three minutes breathing deeply, with the intention of making more room to listen to your body. Allow each inhalation to bring in more inner space and better acoustics for inner listening. Allow each exhalation to release tension and cluttered or disorganized thought.

After three minutes, begin to tonalize the breath with the vocal sound *ah*. Continue to make the *ah* sound on the exhalation for a couple of minutes. Allow the *ah* to be yawn-like. Become aware of the breath within the sound. There is no need to produce a clear *ah*, it can be sleepy and just natural.

"I set out to visit some noteworthy monasteries in Tibet. One was Gyütö Tantric College, whose monks use a remarkable chanting style which sounds as though each participant is singing in chords. Word of Gyütö's chanting had already reached the West, and in scholarly journals, musicologists and acousticians analyzed how the sound is created.

Apparently, Gyütö's members produce low bass notes with unusually rich overtones, so that it sounds as though each participant is producing a chord. But this dry technical description doesn't begin to convey the timeless deep peace which Gyütö's slow-moving melodies evoke."

—David Lewiston, producer of landmark recording of the chants of Tibetan monks

Then allow thoughts about the past twenty-four hours to emerge. As you review the past day, start with this exercise and progress backward through your activities and associations. Begin to observe the emotions that arise when you ask yourself, "Was I heard? Was I understood?" The answer is not a yes or no, but just a non-judgmental sensing. Remember to keep breathing naturally, but deeply with the tonalized *ah*.

Now allow yourself to go deeply into situations you remember when you felt wounded. Think of a time when you felt unheard, unnamed, and frustrated. Go gently into this vulnerable or awkward time and allow the *ah* to fill the place in your body where the wounding occurred. Allow the tonalization of the sound to release the emotion. Use the power of the breath and your own sound to heal that wounding, the pain of that feeling of alienation. Even though you may not have consciously felt the pain at the time of the wounding, release it now with your voice.

Then bring your mind back to a calm place. Use the *ah* to fill your body and mind with a clear and vital sound. You may wish to image the opening of a window on a clear, beautiful day with the *ah* as fresh air clearing the room.

Please reread this exercise at least three times before you begin the exercise. The last section is the most important because it clarifies the experience. When you are finished, stretch and spend a few minutes walking outside, moving to some music or exercising lightly. Give your body time to integrate the rhythms and patterns. Enjoy the resting powers of *ah*.

Exploring Your Body with Your Voice

EXERCISE One of the most interesting ways to investigate the power of the voice is to place the palms of the hands at different places on the body . While comfortably seated, close your eyes and imagine that you are deaf and cannot hear any of the sounds and that your hands are your ears. Being with an *ah* sound as you place your hands on your cheeks. Stay on one comfortable tone for a few minutes, then gradually modify your voice to an *oh* sound. Then spend three minutes on a *eh* sound.

After toning these different vowels, keep the eyes closed and bring your hands to your lap. Breath quietly for a few minutes and notice the shoulders, hands and mind.

Repeat this exercise with the hands on top of the head, then later repeat it with the hands on the heart and chest. Remember to rest after making these tones, and notice the power of the energy inside the sound. This exercise is one of the most relaxing and vitalizing at the same time.

Explore all the vowels in different parts of the body to release tension, stress and pain. If you notice any uncomfortable energy being release, rest for a minute and then return to the *ah* sound. A relaxed jaw is essential in all the toning exercises.

The Sound of Active Peace

Often we think of peace as a passive event where everything is in a subdued state. Peaceful music is often slow without much activity. Yet even when we imagine a beautiful field on a spring day, this is an enormous amount of life orchestrated in harmony. Growth of plants, wind, the power of sunlight and the activities of insects are all moving in their own harmonic fashion with each other. The physical body is similar. Even when we are asleep, the natural rhythms within the body are living.

EXERCISE Sit comfortably with your eyes closed and begin to observe the flow of your breath. After a minute begin to think the word "Peace"with each inhalation and exhalation. Allow the word to extend through your full breath, so that you feel the beauty of the tone in your mind. *Peeeeeeace*. One word per breath. As you breath in, feel the meaning and power of the word "peace" flow in through your breath to the lungs. Then feel the power and peace of the oxygenated blood flow to all parts of your body. As you exhale, think the word "peace" as being released from your mind and body to the space around you.

After a few minutes begin to sound the word as one long tone with each exhalation. Think of it as a vital, living, conscious energy, a state of balanced, vivid harmony between the inner and outer worlds. As you inhale continue to image the feeling and vibration in your body. Allow your mind and body to focus and charge themselves through both the thought and the sound.

Breath and Voice

A few years ago I visited a monastery in southern France, which had been taken over by a new abbot, a young man. He had changed the internal rule of the abbey by modifying everything a little after the Second Vatican Council, and he was therefore something of a revolutionary. When I arrived, there were those who wanted to retain the Latin, others who were for the existing rule, and still others who wanted to change and revolutionize everything. Finally everything was changed. They even eliminated chanting from their daily schedule. You know the Benedictines chant from six to eight hours a day, but this abbot succeeded in demonstrating that chant served no useful purpose, and that without it they could recapture that time for other things.

Well, in fact, these people had been chanting in order to "charge" themselves, but they hadn't realized what they were doing. And gradually, as the days passed, they started to get bogged down; they became more and more tired. Finally they got so tired that they held a meeting and frankly asked themselves what it was that was causing their fatigue. They looked at their schedule and saw that their night vigil and the rhythm of their work deviated excessively from the norm for other men...and they seldom slept. They decided that they should go to bed early and wake up, like everybody else... (but after that) they were more tired than ever. So much so that they called in medical specialists to help them understand what was happening. They finally gave up on this after a procession of doctors had come through over a period of several months, and the monks were more tired than ever. Then they turned to specialists of the digestive system. One of the great French doctors arrived at the conclusion that they were in this state because they were undernourished. In fact, they were practically vegetarian—they ate a little fish from time to time—and he told them they were dying of starvation. I think my colleague's error was in forgetting that they had eaten as vegetarians ever since the twelfth century, which one would think might have engendered some sort of adaptation in them. Anyway, once they started eating meat and potatoes like the rest of the world, things only got worse.

I was called by the abbot in February of 1967, and I found that seventy of the ninety-seven monks were slumping in their cells like wet dish rags. Over the next several months I examined them, installed some machines to electronically reawaken their ears, and reintroduced their chanting immediately. By November, almost all of them had gone back to their normal activities, that is their prayer, their few hours of sleep, and the legendary Benedictine work schedule.

Chanting is a reawakening of the field of consciousness. At the risk of oversimplifying, hypnotic effects are those of relatively lower frequency which play on the more primitive areas of the brain. With Gregorian chant you are directly affecting the cortex, which controls the monkey rather than being led by him.

In order to avoid the awkwardness of having some monks with trained ears and some without, it was best to put them all on the same wavelength immediately. This is the situation you find naturally when they have been singing together for many years. There is an identical rising auditory curve, one which has undoubtedly been conditioned by the sustained breathing they do, and which makes for a unity that is hard to find elsewhere in the world. If you take two monks and charge their ears with opposite curves, they will immediately enter into conflict at the level of language. Thus, Gregorian chant needs perfect blending. If you give this sort of auditory curve to someone who is not a monk, he or she will become extremely aware. It is impossible to arrive at this state of permanent consciousness, though, without having the opportunity always being charged. And of course the environment of the monastery is a very important factor. The Benedictines are lucky in that they are vowed to silence. This is a verbal silence which keeps one from uttering conscious nonsense. But it is important, if you succeed in extricating yourself from this condition, that a strong stimulus be provided—for at least four and a half hours each day as I said—in order that one can meditate or work. That is what chant is doing.

In the past some monks believed Gregorian was to be sung like lyric songs. They pushed very hard and sang Gregorian as if they were singing Othello. But this is false because Gregorian is meant to train one to rise up out of the body. To give a sense of interiority, yes, but an interiority in the cosmos itself.

(excerpt from an interview with Dr. Alfred Tomatis in *The Roar of Silence*, by Don G.Campbell, Quest Books.)

CHAPTER 6

Music for Relaxation

Kay Gardner

Kay Gardner ~ composer, teacher and recording artist ~ is the author of *Sounding the Inner Landscape: Music As Medicine*. For the past twenty years, she has been among a vanguard of composers creating music designed for meditation, relaxation and healing. Gardner has released a dozen recordings of original music ~ from solo flute meditations to large orchestral and choral compositions, and her works have been performed by ensembles throughout the United States and Europe. Kay Gardner travels globally leading workshops and lecturing at colleges and universities. When at home in Maine she spends her time composing, writing and leading the chorus, "Women With Wings."

*A*t the nursing home where I went from room to room entertaining residents with my flute, there was a woman in her eighties suffering from Alzheimer's Disease. Her name was Sophie, and she wandered the halls slowly, supporting herself with two canes. Her eyes had a glazed, uncomprehending look. But as soon as she heard the jaunty flute tunes I played as I walked down the hall, she lifted both her canes, became bright-eyed and danced a little jig. When the music stopped, Sophie resumed her stooped shuffle with canes, and the sparkle in her eyes left.

Whether subtle or overwhelming (as in the above example) music possesses great powers to affect change. Some music stirs us up; some music slows us down. Some music invites us to dance; other music soothes us to sleep. Without even being conscious of it, we are all affected by the music we are exposed to every day. Knowing what it is in music that has the power to move us enables us to consciously choose music to relax by.

THE ROLE OF MUSIC IN OUR LIVES

As long as humans have had voices, humans have made music for healing. In less technologically-advanced cultures, accompanying themselves on sticks, rocks and bones, medicine men and women call to the spirits for healing.

In ancient Greece, India, China and Egypt, when flutes and plucked string instruments came into use, healing incantations were chanted by the priestesses and priests. During the European medieval times, physicians were required to study music as essential to medicine, especially for recognizing the rhythms of the body's pulses. After the Renaissance, as the nature of music became more complex, it became more an aesthetic expression and less a functional one. Keyboards and bowed string instruments were used, but music wasn't used specifically for healing; it was used almost exclusively for performance.

Today, after over three centuries of neglect, the functional aspects of music are experiencing a revival; they now complement music's aesthetic role. Music for healing and relaxation is again being created vocally, on acoustic instruments and on modern electronic instruments, like the synthesizer.

What is it about music that makes it healing or relaxing? A better understanding will help us to become more attuned to our environment and to the sounds we're exposed to every day.

Listening

EXERCISE Close your eyes and get in touch with where your breathing comes from. Without judgment, begin to recognize the sounds in your immediate external surroundings. Allow each sound to enter your consciousness one by one, each like a differently colored thread. Now tune in to distant sounds. Add these threads to your aural loom. Lastly, go within and listen to the sounds of your body. Add these sounds to the rich tapestry of sounds you have already recognized. Allow the sounds to flow together in your consciousness, creating your own original composition. Spend some time with the sounds, and when you are ready, come back to awareness of your immediate sur-roundings, relaxed.

Today we are offered music in virtually every setting ~ at home, at work, on vacation. Music plays in elevators and gro-cery stores, in doctors' offices and health spas, in commercials on radio and TV, at athletic events, in hospitals, at camp-grounds, anywhere people are gathered for any purpose. Even if we wanted to, we'd be unable to avoid music. For the most part, we're unaware of how our senses are inundated with constant sound and music.

Still, we can choose to use music to enhance our everyday lives. Music can calm and center us in stressful situations; music can relax us at the end of long work days. Relaxing music may be listened to while we're having dental work done or even while we're having major surgery.

When we listen to music, we usually hear it as an entirety. We don't sit and analyze all the different elements of the music to figure out why it has an effect on us. But if we did take the music apart element by element ~ the rhythm is doing this, the melody is doing that ~ we'd realize that each element in itself can have an individual relaxing effect.

Understanding the Elements of Music

In choosing music for relaxation, it is helpful to know how music can be broken down, how each part of it can contribute to the whole. Of the following musical elements each may be healing in itself. Alone or together, these elements contribute to our relaxation.

Drone

When the wind blows steadily through telephone wires, it sets up a drone sound. This uninterrupted, steady drone can be very relaxing. Why? Because drones create a steady vibration or a resonance in the body. When a particular part of the body is vibrated, it's being massaged from within. The ancient Sanskrit mantra *Om* is the most centering and relaxing word in the world. When chanted as a drone either alone or with a group, the *Om,* because of its special characteristics, massages every organ and every system in the body.

EXERCISE Close your eyes and get in touch with where your breathing comes from. Without judging how you sound, take a deep breath and begin intoning the word *Om*. Exaggerate the length of the word, drawing each syllable out—*Ah......Oh.....Mmmmmmmmmmmm*. In between each , *Om,* inhale, exhale and inhale again. Allow your *Om*s to be long and deep. Be aware of how and where the drone of the *Om* touches within your body. Be aware if any other subtle sounds decorate the basic sound of your *Om*. Spend some time with your *Om,* and when you're ready, come back to your immediate surroundings, relaxed.

Of all the instruments available to humankind, our own voices are the most accessible and potentially the most relaxing. Very often we can find ourselves tightening or tensing certain parts of our bodies, sometimes not even aware that we're doing it. Droning on individual vowels can create resonance and relaxation in specific parts of our bodies.

The *Ooo* sound may be used to relax the base of the spine, the sacroiliac and surrounding areas. The *Oh* vowel relaxes the belly area. To relax the diaphragm and its internal organs, drone on

> "What is it that my whole body really expects of music? I believe, its own *ease*: as if all animal functions should be quickened by easy, bold, exuberant, self-assured rhythms; as if iron, leaden life should be gilded by good, golden and tender harmonies. My melancholy wants to rest in the hiding places and abysses of *perfection*: that is why I need music.
>
> —Friedrich Nietzche

the syllable *Aw*. The chest/heart/lung area resonates with the sound *Ah*. Droning on *Eh* relaxes the throat and neck; *Ih* (as in the word "if") relaxes the sinuses, eyes and temples; and *Eee* vibrates the crown of the head.

Repeat the above *Om* exercise substituting each vowel sound for the mantra *Om*.

There are musical instruments that drone, and while their sounds may not be quite as relaxing as your own vocal drones, they too ~ played or heard live or on recording ~ may be used for relaxation.

The most obvious drone instruments are the bagpipes. While Scottish bagpipes are not particularly relaxing, bagpipes from Ireland, Greece or Arabian countries are. The *didjeridoo* (pron: dij-er-ee-*doo*), an Aboriginal instrument from Australia, gives an incredible drone that's almost as completely centering as droning *Om* with your voice. There are a number of recordings featuring the *didjeridoo*. In India, the *tamboura* is the drone instrument you hear at the beginning and all the way through their classical music (*ragas*). Its main purpose is to get the listeners vibrating in sync with it and each other before the melody and rhythm instruments come in above it. Synthesizers and organs can drone quite simply merely by pressing down keys or pedals, and bowed stringed instruments can create drones as well. Any one of these instruments ~ depending upon the tone it plays and for how long ~ can relax different parts of the body.

Repetition

When phrases of words or music are repeated over and over again, like chants or the choruses to pop songs, we become familiar with the tunes, and when we are familiar enough with things, we become comfortable with them. With comfort comes relaxation.

In the 1980s there was a 250-year-old piece of music that seemed to be played everywhere. It was used in commercials; it was played at weddings; it was background music for stretching and yoga classes; and it was used as the theme music for the film "Ordinary People." This composition, Canon in D by Pachelbel, was basically only a sequence of eight bass

An Australian Aboriginal man plays the didjeridoo.

notes repeated twenty-seven times with different variations on top of them. To many listeners, the Pachelbel Canon was one of the most relaxing pieces of music they'd ever heard.

Like the Pachelbel Canon, there are many musical works from classics to pop that include repetition. This music, because of its familiarity, has the effect of relaxing the listener. If the tune has words, and those words are of a comforting nature, the relaxation effect is even stronger.

If your favorite music is classical, you may choose to relax to canons or fugues or *passacaglia* from the Baroque period. Composers in the Classical (Mozart) and Romantic (Beethoven) periods wrote Themes and Variations, exploring, varying, and repeating themes. Skipping to this century's composed music, the Minimalists (Terry Riley, Steve Reich, Philip Glass, among others) built their music on repetition; sometimes a phrase is repeated for up to twenty minutes before a shift occurs. In this case, the purpose is to jog the listener into an altered state of consciousness, but the initial effect can be very relaxing.

The greatest influence on popular music, except for ballads, has been rhythm-and-blues, music that has evolved from African call-and-response chanting. The choruses of these songs are repeated over and over again. If the message of the song is positive and the music not overly loud or energetic, the repetitions can be relaxing.

During the mid-1970s a new kind of music evolved. It came to be called New Age music, and its purpose was specifically to relax and heal the listener. This music, like Minimalist classical music, contains much repetition. In fact, some of the recordings are extended vocal chants that have been orchestrated similarly to Pachelbel's Canon.

World music and ethnic music, that is, music from cultures other than ours, often has much repetition. *Ragas* from India, Irish dance music, chants from African and Asian religions, South American panpipe music, all are types of music that can be relaxing, depending upon their tempos and instrumentation. Though this music may be an acquired taste for some, listeners will be rewarded if they acclimate themselves to the music of global cultures.

EXERCISE Close your eyes and get in touch with where your breathing comes from. Pick a tune you already are familiar with, such as Pachelbel's Canon or a chant that seems to want to repeat itself in your mind's ear. Allow the melody to "play" in your imagination. Playing it over and over again, let it lull you, center you, and relax you. When you have spent some time with your repeated melody, come back to awareness of your immediate surroundings, relaxed.

Chanting word phrases over and over again may be even more relaxing and meditative than listening to repetitious music. In India and Tibet, single word utterances are called mantras. Often they are sacred syllables from the ancient Sanskrit language and are meant to transport chanters to more relaxed states of mind and body. These "magic" words are chanted over and over again, sometimes slowly, sometimes quickly. The repetition acts as a kind of self hypnosis, relaxing the chanter.

EXERCISE Close your eyes and get in touch with where your breathing comes from. Pick a series of positive words, words of self-empowerment or affirmation, and repeat them over and over again silently or aloud. Repeat the words until they no longer make sense, becoming merely connected sounds. Let the words lull you, center you, and relax you. When you have spent some time with your word-sounds, come back to awareness of your immediate surroundings, relaxed.

Pulse/Rhythm

When the rhythm of the music we're listening to is duplicating our bodily pulses at rest, we are the most relaxed. Though there are many different pulses in our bodies, those most obvious to us are our heartbeats and our breath cycles. Less obvious, but very important, are our brain waves.

When we are exposed to loud, rhythmic music, we automatically begin to sway to the rhythm, tapping our toes or clapping our hands to the beat. We humans are very rhythmic animals, and because of this, our pulses begin to beat with the rhythms we are exposed to. Either our heartbeats throb in sync with the beat, or our breath cycles move with the rhythm. On a more subtle level, our brain waves dance with music as well.

When choosing music to help us relax, we should keep the heartbeat in mind. Loud rock music, with a beat that is not in sync with our hearts, can make us weak and irritable. Frenetic jazz pieces with constantly-changing rhythms are not conducive to relaxation either. In classical music, late 19th Century works by such composers as Wagner and Strauss, may be too emotionally overwrought to be used for relaxation. Using the healthy heartbeat (at fifty to eighty beats per minute) as a basis for choosing our relaxation music, we may be directed to selections that will slow us down and put us in a gentler frame of mind.

Today's record shelves offer a large assortment of CDs and cassettes with sounds and music designed to slow our pulses down so that we may relax. The Lind Institute has a series of tapes of the slow movements from Baroque and Classical works. Called "Relax with the Classics," these are high-quality performances by noted American and European orchestras playing music pulsing at the rhythms of the heartbeat at rest. People going into surgery find these tapes very relaxing, but they are equally relaxing, if not more so, for ordinary listening.

Harmony

Harmony is what creates moods in music. Listening to music with simple, pleasant harmonies is much more relaxing than listening to dissonant, jarring harmonies. Gregorian chants are built on one of the most relaxing intervals in music, and can be used to settle our emotions and our spirits.

EXERCISE In your tape recorder, record yourself chanting a drone sound. Keep on that same basic drone for a good long time. Now, rewind to the beginning of your tape and play what you've just recorded. While it's playing, drone another sound above it. (You have created what in music is called an "interval." An interval is the space between your two drone sounds; intervals are the simplest characteristics of harmony.) Observe how the interval you've created affects you. Is it relaxing? Is it disturbing?

KAY GARDNER

Make another drone sound. And another. And another until you find the interval that is most relaxing for you. Stay with this harmonious interval for a good long time, then return to awareness of your immediate surroundings, relaxed.

Melody

Have you ever listened to a gorgeous piece of instrumental music and found yourself transported? The music ends, and you realize that you were out beyond awareness of your physical body? Melody has the power to lift us up. Because of this, listening to melodious music can be extremely relaxing. When we are in that high, transcendent place, we are not aware of the stresses and anxieties we may live with every day. We are, for the time the music is playing, free!

Each world culture or society has special series of tones (scales) that make up its melodies. In primitive times, melodies were developed from the sounds of the environment, such as rain on hollow logs or the sound of the wind blowing through desert, jungle, plains, ice fields, forests, or beaches. Creature sounds and the sounds of people working also contributed to the tones that made up special scales and melodies.

The ancient Greek scales were called modes, and each one of the seven modes they used had a different effect on the listener. Melodies in these modes could evoke sadness or happiness, serenity or excitement. Many of these modes continue to be used in Appalachian folk music, in Balkan songs, and in the classical works of Bartok and Vaughn Williams.

In Indian classical music, there are over 5,000 different melodic scales (*ragas*). Each has a specific purpose and a particular effect. There are devotional *ragas*, *ragas* for the seasons of the year, *ragas* for different times of the day, *ragas* for work, and *ragas* for relaxation. I find the music recorded by the flutist Sachdev especially relaxing, especially his "Romantic Ragas," and "Master of the Bamboo Flute" on the Chandi label.

Opening ourselves up to music from different cultures can increase the potential for relaxation as we learn to appreciate the different melodies and their effects. Rather than just playing music as background, consciously use melodious music for stress reduction and relaxation.

 **EXERCISE** Put a favorite instrumental recording on your player. Close your eyes and get in touch with where your breathing comes from. As the music plays, be aware of your toes. Relax your toes. One at a time, come to awareness of your shins, then your knees, thighs, pelvis, belly, diaphragm, chest, neck, face, and brain. Relax each in turn until your entire body is completely relaxed. When you are relaxed, disappear into the melody. Let it take you with it. You may see visions or images. You may just float above consciousness until the music ends. When the music finishes, return to awareness of your immediate surroundings, relaxed and refreshed.

Instrumental Color

If you were asked where in your body you felt the sound of a flute, where would you point? Where would you point if you were asked where the tuba resonated in you? What about the string orchestra? Guitar? Harp? Wind chimes? Drums? Each instrument or family of instruments ~ woodwinds, brasses, strings and percussion ~ will touch us in a particular part of our bodies. Like the drone, musical instruments, when chosen consciously, can relax specific parts of our bodies that tend to hold tension.

When you are choosing recorded music for relaxation, be aware of your own special needs. You wouldn't listen to drum music if you had a headache and needed to relax. You wouldn't choose flute music if you were feeling somewhat spacey or ungrounded. Deep brass music wouldn't soothe you if your diaphragm or chest were feeling tight, but the music from a string orchestra might help relieve that tension and let you move into relaxation.

A recording that can familiarize you with the sounds of the different families of instruments is Benjamin Britten's "A Young Person's Guide to the Orchestra." There are many recorded versions of this piece available. Each orchestral instrument is featured alone and with its family of instrumental relatives. While listening to this recording, close your eyes and let the sounds of these different instruments touch your mind and body. Note which instruments you relate to, which instruments cause stress in you, and which instruments relax you. When choosing recorded music for relaxation, keep the effects of the different instruments in mind.

EXERCISE Put a favorite instrumental recording on your player. Close your eyes and get in touch with where your breathing comes from. Locate the sound of the flute.

Allow the sound to travel inside you with your breath. As you are hearing the sound of the flute, be aware of what part of your body the flute sound travels to. When you have identified the area, hold it in your memory, and move on. Now, identify the part of your body that holds the most tension. (It could be your shoulders; it could be your neck; wherever your stress finds itself settling in your body.) Identify which of your recording's musical instruments vibrates the part of your body that holds stress. Allow that instrument's sound to travel to the place of your physical tension. Allow the sound of that instrument to resonate you, soothing you and calming you. When you have spent enough time with the sound to notice a relaxation, return to awareness of your immediate surroundings, relaxed and refreshed.

Practicing the above exercise may help you relax your body's tense areas, but choosing recorded music that features your chosen instruments may be just as effective.

Loudness/Softness

During the sixties and seventies, there was a teenage fad of taking soft-boiled eggs to rock concerts, placing them on the edge of the stage, and finding them hard-boiled at the concert's intermission. Loud, shrill sounds sent into liquids have been found to coagulate protein.

Some rock groups specifically asked that listeners turn up the volume on their recordings. In live concert these same groups cranked up their sound systems to very high decibel levels. The purpose of the loudness, according to some of these musicians, was to numb the listeners. But, if loud sounds can cook eggs and change the makeup of protein, what would these loud sounds be doing to our bodies? They may be numbing us, but they certainly would not be relaxing us.

In choosing relaxing music, you will probably wish to listen to music that is at a comfortable level of sound. The sound should not be attacking your eardrums (or your body) in any painful way.

CHOOSING YOUR OWN MUSIC TO RELAX TO

Understanding and using the musical elements described above will give you the skills to choose music that is just right for you. Remember, each element alone has relaxing characteristics, but when blended together in songs or compositions, more than one element can contribute to your state of relaxation.

Which kind of music you choose for relaxation will entirely depend upon your personal taste in music. Soft rock may not be relaxing to a classical music lover. Jazz may not be a medium that relaxes someone who likes country music. The relaxing elements of music are present in all music to some degree or another. Choose what works for you.

There are types of music, other than New Age, Classical and World/Ethnic music mentioned earlier, that are helpful for relaxing. Ambient or background music ~ or as the composer Satie called it, "wallpaper music" ~ may be played in the work place or at home to help set a relaxing atmosphere. Doctors' offices often play ambient music to soothe nervous patients. Overdoing ambient music ~ like the Muzak in grocery stores ~ is not particularly relaxing. This is because it is monotonous and there is usually no break at all. We need a small stretch of silence every twenty minutes or so, or stress begins to build again.

Environmental sounds are now available on recordings, and are used by many people for relaxation. There are several series of environmental sound recordings. The Environments Series includes tapes called "Heartbeat," "English Meadow," and "Country Stream." The Solitudes Series offers the listener "Dawn on the Desert," "On a Wilderness Lake," among other titles. The steady rhythms and sounds of Nature are immediately soothing and settling and wonderful to relax to.

In India, it is said, the universe hangs on sound. Not ordinary sound, but a cosmic vibration so massive and subtle and all-encompassing that everything seen and unseen (including man) is filled with it.

—Fritjof Capra,
The Tao of Physics
(Bantam)

CREATING YOUR OWN RELAXATION MUSIC

In the exercises describing the musical elements, you already created vocal sounds that contribute to relaxation. You also experienced sacred sounds in the form of the mantra *Om*. In many, many communities you will find groups of people who like to chant or sing. There are church and community choruses everywhere, and choir members are convinced that singing with others is invigorating as well as calming. If you relate more to chanting, you may wish to join the meditation groups connected with Eastern and Native American spiritual practices. These groups meet in large cities or at rural retreats to chant together on a regular basis. Your own voice has the potential of being the most relaxing instrument of all. Use it. Enjoy it. Relax with it.

If you play a musical instrument, you may also want to experiment with the elements to create your own original relaxation pieces. For example, if you play keyboard, set up a repeated pattern in your left (bass) hand. Let its rhythm duplicate the healthy heartbeat. Lub-dub-pause. Lub-dub-pause. Add a simple harmony, using intervals you find soothing. Now add a melody line with your right hand. Don't worry about whether it sounds "right." Loosen your body. Let the music flow into its own shape. Experiment. Play. Enjoy. Relax.

NEGATIVE EFFECTS OF SOUND/MUSIC

How can we relax when we are being assaulted by sounds in our work places, in our homes, and on our streets and highways? Such subtle sounds as those of defective florescent light bulbs, or refrigerator hums can be subliminal stress-makers. The squeal of tires on roads, the honking of car horns on city streets, the rat-a-tat sounds of jackhammers on cement are disturbing to us as are the sounds of children screaming, construction sounds, overhead airplanes, neighbors' stereos, subways, and office machinery.

When subjected to these disturbing sounds day after day after day, we become tense and irritable. We need to be able to counteract the effects of these sounds so that we can function at our best. First, if you notice that there is an objectionable sound at your work place and you can do something about it, make no hesitation. Have that florescent light bulb replaced. Get a foam pad to put under the refrigerator or other noisy machine in office or home. This will deaden some of the sound. See if you can get your work place to install acoustical ceiling tiles and wallboard and carpeting to keep the disturbing sounds from above, below and around you to a dull roar.

Using Music as a Relaxation Tool

In the morning, rather than having a bell or buzzer wake you up, begin your day with a musical awakening. Set your clock radio to a station that plays easy music. This may not work for heavy sleepers, but it starts the day more gently for those who wish to keep their stress levels down.

While getting ready for work, play music that has energy but isn't chaotic (uptempo ballads, Bach, laid-back jazz, soft rock). If your drive to the work place takes you through noisy traffic or past loud construction sites, play music in your car that you like to sing with, chants or popular songs. The resonance of the music and your own voice will mask the extraneous noise.

If you work in an office, ask if you can wear a Walkman while at your desk. Listen to your favorite soothing music, or to environmental music. Listening to an English meadow while typing a report will definitely keep your stress level down.

These days most factories play music all day long for workers on all shifts, but workers don't usually have a say in what kind of music is played. This can be a problem, because not everyone likes the same kinds of music. If using your ears isn't part of your factory job, ask the management to allow workers to wear Walkmen. Here, too, you'll want to mask the annoying factory sounds with music that keeps you energized but doesn't make you frantic.

When you return home after a long day of work, try to take a half hour to sit in a chair or lie on the couch with headphones on playing a recording of repetitious music, such as the extended chant music of Kim Robertson or Robert Gass, the recordings offered by "Relax with the Classics," or the venerable Canon by Pachelbel. Headphones have the unique ability to immerse you in the music, to so fill your head with the sound that everything else, including stress, drops away. Consciously relax your body as you listen.

If you don't have headphones, turn your stereo or tuner up loud enough so that you can hear it in the bathroom, and let your immersion be in a warm bath accompanied by the relaxing music. Or, if your stereo speakers are on the floor, lie down on that floor and let the vibrations resonate your entire body, like a sonic massage.

When you go to bed, if your daily activities are bouncing around in your thoughts, there are three things you can do. You can focus in on chanting an *Om* either aloud or in your mind's ear; you can tune your radio to the easy station you wake to in the morning; or you can play an environmental tape of ocean surf or a waterfall, sounds that are especially conducive to rest and relaxation.

THE GIFT OF MUSIC

Music is a wonderful gift with powers to heal and calm us. Take time to recognize the relaxing and healing elements in the music you listen to, and wisely choose music to accompany you through the day, helping you to release your tension and stress so that you may function at your highest potential.

The 1,000-Year Overnight Sensation

Hits and hitmakers come and go, but some stand out. Take the case of "Chant," an album of Gregorian melodies sung by Benedictine monks from their 11th-century monastery in the abbey of Santo Domingo de Silos in Spain.

Issued, appropriately enough, by Angel Records, "Chant" began as a surprise hit in Spain, selling over 200,000 copies in that country alone. Since its US. and international release, Chant has sold over 2 million copies, easily outselling all classical music albums, and soaring to the Top Ten among pop hits for 1994. Perhaps even more surprising, "Chant" found its way to alternative rock radio and even MTV; research showed that most buyers were between the ages of 16 and 25.

"The basic appeal of the album," said Father Jerome Weber, a Catholic priest and an expert on chant, "is simplicity, purity and mysticism. There is an intuition of the beyond, both in the recording and in the way people are hearing it."

"A psalm implies serenity of soul, it is the author of peace, which calms bewildering thoughts," wrote St. Basil, who founded the Christian monastic movement. More recently, Rafael Perez-Arroyo, general manager of EMI Classics—who first struck gold with the Spanish edition of Chant—told reporters for *Billboard* magazine that he marketed the recording as "a solution to traffic jams, telephones and other modern pressures."

It appears that despite all the new music around our radio dials—from rock to reggae, classical to jazz, contemporary listeners needed to look back nearly 13 centuries to find some peace. Of course, for the Benedcitine monks, this sudden brush with stardom was less than relaxing. "You have to understand," one was quoted to say, "we are monks, not rock stars."

CHAPTER 7

Creative Visualization

Shakti Gawain

Shakti Gawain is a best-selling author and an internationally renowned speaker and workshop leader in the world consciousness movement. *The Path of Trans-formation: How Healing Ourselves Can Change the World*, her newest book is the latest in a distinguished line of published works exploring the human potential. Among Shakti Gawain's titles, her landmark work, *Creative Visualization*, has more than two million copies in print;

Living In the Light has sold over 700,000 copies. Through her writing, seminars and workshops, Shakti has helped a worldwide audience to act on their own intuition and creativity.

Shakti Gawain co-founded Nataraj Publishing with her husband Jim Burns and was co-founder of New World Library publishing company. She and her husband make their home in Mill Valley, California, and on the island of Kauai, Hawaii.

Gawain has appeared on such nationally syndicated shows as *The Oprah Winfrey Show*, *Good Morning America*, *Sonya Live* on CNN, *The Larry King Show*, and *New Dimensions Radio*.

The problem of how to find relaxation is probably one of the biggest challenges that we in modern Western civilization face. We have such an external focus in our lives; there are so many things vying for our attention. Our culture is concentrated almost exclusively on the "doing" aspect of life, and not the "being." As a result, we are losing our ability to relax. We need to relearn this skill. We need to learn to balance the amount of time we spend that is goal-oriented--doing, pushing, accomplishing--with some time in the being mode, where we're able to relax and replenish ourselves. We need to embrace another kind of energy.

When we are truly relaxed, we exist in the most nurturing of states. It's healthy for our bodies, it's nourishing emotionally, and it is restful for our minds. It also presents a place from which we can find a deeper spiritual connection.

It is equally true that when we are relaxed, we feel more fulfilled, alive and creative, and we are capable of achieving more.

For me, relaxation has to do with learning to consciously make that shift from doing to being mode. Creative visualization can help us learn this skill. It provides exercises to practice and refine our ability to make that shift.

If you practice creative visualization as outlined in this chapter, you will automatically learn how to relax more frequently and more regularly in your own life--it is a process that naturally encourages relaxation.

WHAT IS CREATIVE VISUALIZATION?

Creative visualization is the technique of using your imagination to create what you want in your life. There is nothing at all new, strange, or unusual about creative visualization. You are already using it every day, every minute in fact. It is your natural power of imagination, the basic creative energy of the universe which you use constantly, whether or not you are aware of it.

In the past, many of us have used our power of creative visualization in a relatively unconscious way. Because of our own deep-seated negative concepts about life, we have automatically and unconsciously expected and imagined lack, limitation, difficulties, and problems to be our lot in life. To one degree or another that is what we have created for ourselves.

This chapter is about learning to use your natural creative imagination in a more and more conscious way, as a technique to create what you truly want — love, fulfillment, enjoyment, satisfying relationships, rewarding work, self-expression, health, beauty, prosperity, inner peace and harmony... whatever your heart desires. The use of creative visualization gives us a key to tap into the natural goodness and bounty of life.

Imagining Your Goals

Imagination is the ability to create an idea or metal picture in your mind. In creative visualization you use your imagination to create a clear image of something you wish to manifest. Then you continue to focus on the idea or picture regularly, giving it positive energy until it becomes objective reality ... in other words, until you actually achieve what you have been visualizing.

Your goal may be on any level — physical, emotional, mental, or spiritual. You might imagine yourself with a new home, or a new job, or having a beautiful relationship, or feeling calm and serene, or perhaps with an improved memory and learning ability. Or you might picture yourself handling a difficult situation effortlessly, or simple see yourself as a radiant being, filled with light and love. You can work on any level, and all will have results... through experience you will find the particular images and techniques which work best for you.

Let us say, for example, that you have difficulty getting along with someone and you would like to create a more harmonious relationship with that person.

After relaxing into a deep, quiet, meditative state of mind, you mentally imagine the two of you relating and communicating in an open, honest, and harmonious way. Try to get a feeling in yourself that your mental image is possible; experience it as if it is already happening.

Repeat this short, simple exercise often, perhaps two or three times a day or whenever you think about it. If you are sincere in your desire and intention, and truly open to change, you will soon find that the relationship is becoming easier and more flowing, and that the other person seems to become more agreeable and easier to communicate with. Eventually, you will find that the problem will resolve itself completely, in one way or another, to the benefit of all parties concerned.

It should be noted here that this technique cannot be used to "control" the behavior of others or cause them to do something against their will. Its effect is to dissolve our internal barriers to natural harmony and self-realization, allowing everyone to manifest in their most positive aspect.

To use creative visualization it is not necessary to believe in any metaphysical or spiritual ideas, though you must be willing to entertain certain concepts as being possible. It is not necessary to "have faith" in any power outside yourself. The only thing necessary is that you have the desire to enrich your knowledge and experience, and an open enough mind to try something new in a positive spirit. Study the principles, try the techniques with an open mind and heart, and then judge for yourself whether they are useful to you.

If so, continue using and developing them, and soon the changes in yourself and your life will probably exceed anything you could have originally dreamed of.

Creative visualization is magic in the truest and highest meaning of the word. It involves understanding and aligning yourself with the natural principles that govern the workings of our universe, and learning to use these principles in the most conscious and creative way.

If you had never seen a gorgeous flower or a spectacular sunset before, and someone described one to you, you might consider it to be a miraculous thing (which it truly is!). Once you saw a few yourself, and began to learn something about the natural laws involved, you would begin to understand how they are formed and it would seem natural to you and not particularly mysterious.

The same is true of the process of creative visualization. What at first might seem amazing or impossible to the very limited type of education our rational minds have received, becomes perfectly understandable once we learn and practice with the underlying concepts involved.

Once you do so, it may seem that you are working miracles in your life... and you truly will be!

How Creative Visualization Works

In order to understand how creative visualization works, it's useful to look are several interrelated principles:

The Physical Universe is Energy

The scientific world is beginning to discover what metaphysical and spiritual teachers have known for centuries. Our physical universe is not really composed of any "matter" at all; its basic component is a kind of force or essence which we can call energy.

Things appear to be solid and separate from one another on the level at which our physical senses normally perceive them. On finer levels, however, atomic and subatomic levels, seemingly solid matter is seen to be smaller and smaller particles within particles, which eventually turn out to be just pure energy.

Physically, we are all energy, and everything within and around us is made up of energy. We are all part of one great energy field. Things which we perceive to be solid and separate are in reality just various forms of our essential energy which is common to all. We are all one, even in a literal, physical sense.

The energy is vibrating at different rates of speed, and thus has different qualities, from finer to denser. Thought is a relatively fine, light form of energy and therefore very quick and easy to change. Matter is relatively dense, compact energy, and therefore slower to move and change. Within matter there is great variation as well. Living flesh is relatively fine, changes quickly, and is easily affected by many things. A rock is a much denser form, slower to change and more difficult to affect. Yet even rock is eventually changed and affected by the fine, light energy of water, for example. All forms of energy are interrelated and can affect one another.

Energy is Magnetic

One law of energy is this: energy of a certain quality or vibration tends to attract energy of a similar quality and vibration.

Thought and feelings have their own magnetic energy which attracts energy of similar nature. We can see this principle at work, for instance, when we "accidentally" run into someone we've just been thinking of, or "happen" to pick up a book which contains exactly the perfect information we need at that moment.

Form Follows Idea

Thought is a quick, light, mobile form of energy. It manifests instantaneously, unlike the dense forms such as matter.

When we create something, we always create it first in a thought form. A thought or idea always precedes manifestation. "I think I'll make dinner" is the idea which precedes creation of a meal. "I want a new dress," precedes going and buying one; "I need a job" precedes finding one, and so on.

An artist first has an idea or inspiration, then creates a painting. A builder first has a design, then builds a house.

The idea is like a blueprint; it creates an image of the form, which then magnetizes and guides the physical energy to flow into that form and eventually manifests it on the physical plane.

The same principle holds true even if we do not take direct physical action to manifest or ideas. Simply having an idea or thought, holding it in your mind, is an energy which will tend to attract and create that form on the material plane. If you constantly think of illness, you eventually become ill; if you believe yourself to be beautiful, you become so.

THE LAW OF RADIATION AND ATTRACTION

This is the principle that whatever you put out into the universe will be reflected back to you. "As you sow, so shall you reap."

What this means from a practical standpoint is that we always attract into our lives whatever we think about the most, believe in most strongly, expect on the deepest levels, and/or imagine most vividly.

When we are negative and fearful, insecure or anxious we will tend to attract the very experiences, situations, or people that we are seeking to avoid. If we are basically positive in attitude, expecting and envisioning pleasure, satisfaction and happiness, we will attract and create people, situations, and events which conform to our positive expectations. So the more positive energy we put into imagining what we want, the more it begins to manifest in our lives.

USING CREATIVE VISUALIZATION

The process of change does not occur on superficial levels, through mere "positive thinking." It involves exploring, discovering, and changing our deepest, most basic attitudes toward life. That is why learning to use creative visualization can become a process of deep and meaningful growth. In the process we often discover ways in which we have been holding ourselves back, blocking ourselves from achieving satisfaction and fulfillment in life through our fears and negative concepts. Once seen clearly, these limiting attitudes can be dissolved through the creative visualization process, leaving space for us to find and live our natural state of happiness, fulfillment, and love...

At first you may practice creative visualization at specific times and for specific goals. As you get more in the habit of using it, and begin to trust the results it can bring you, you will find that it becomes an integral part of your thinking process. It becomes a continuous awareness, a state of consciousness in which you know that you are the constant creator of your life.

That is the ultimate point of creative visualization — to make every moment of our lives a moment of wondrous creation, in which we are just naturally choosing the best, the most beautiful, the most fulfilling lives we can imagine...

A Simple Exercise in Creative Visualization

Here's an exercise in the basic technique of creative visualization:

EXERCISE First, think of something you would like. For this exercise choose something simple, that you can easily imagine attaining. It might be an object you would like to have, an event you'd like to happen, a situation in which you'd like to find yourself, or some circumstance in your life which you'd like to improve.

Get in a comfortable position, either sitting or lying down, in a quiet place where you won't be disturbed. Relax your body completely. Starting from your toes and moving up to your scalp, think of relaxing each muscle in your body in turn, letting all tension flow our of your body. Breathe deeply and slowly, from your belly. Count down slowly from 10 to 1, feeling yourself getting more deeply relaxed with each count.

When you feel deeply relaxed, start to imagine the thing your want exactly as you would like it. If it is an object, imagine yourself with the object, using it, admiring it, enjoying it, showing it to friends. If it is a situation or event, imagine yourself there and everything happening just as you want it to. You may imagine what people are saying, or any details that make it more real to you.

You may take a relatively short time or quite a few minutes to imagine this — whatever feels best to you. Have fun with it. It should be a thoroughly enjoyable experience, like a child daydreaming about what he wants for his birthday.

Now keeping the idea or image still in your mind, mentally make some very positive, affirmative statements to yourself (aloud or silently, as you prefer) about it, such as:

"Here I am spending a wonderful weekend in the mountains. What a beautiful vacation," or:

"I now have a wonderful, happy relationship with _____. We are really learning to understand each other."

These positive statements, called affirmations, are a very important part of creative visualization, which we will discuss in more detail later.

Always end your visualization with the firm statement to yourself: "This, or something better, now manifests for me in totally satisfying and harmonious ways, for the highest good of all concerned."

This leaves room for something different and even better than you had originally envisioned to happen, and serves as a reminder to you that this process only functions for the mutual benefit of all.

If doubts or contradictory thoughts arise, don't resist them or try to prevent them. This will tend to give them a power they don't otherwise have. Just let them flow through your consciousness, and return to your positive statements and images.

Do this process only as long as you find it enjoyable and interesting. It could be five minutes or half an hour. Repeat every day, or as often as you can.

As you see, the basic process is relatively simple. To use it really effectively, however, usually requires some understanding and refinement.

HOW TO VISUALIZE

Many people wonder exactly what is meant by the term "visualize." Some worry because they don't actually "see" a mental picture or image when they close their eyes and try to visualize.

Don't get stuck on the term "visualize." It is not at all necessary to mentally see an image. Some people say they see very clear, sharp images when they close their eyes and imagine something. Others feel that they don't really "see" anything, they just sort of "think about" it or imagine that they are looking at it, or become aware of a feeling or impression. That's perfectly fine. We all use our imaginations constantly, it's impossible not to, so whatever process you find yourself doing when you imagine, is fine.

If you still don't feel sure what it means to visualize, read through each of these exercises, then close your eyes and try it:

Close your eyes and relax deeply. Think of some familiar room such as your bedroom or living room. Remember some familiar details of it, such as the color of the carpet, the way the furniture is arranged, how bright or dark it is. Imagine yourself walking into the room and sitting or lying down on a comfortable chair, couch or bed.

Now recall some pleasant experience you have had in the last few days, especially one involving good physical sensations such as eating a delicious meal, receiving a massage, swimming in cool water, or making love. Remember the experience as vividly as possible, and enjoy the pleasurable sensations once again.

Now imagine that you are in some idyllic country setting, perhaps relaxing on soft green grass beside a cool river, or wandering through a beautiful, lush forest. It can be a place that you have been, or an ideal place where you would like to go. Think of the details, and create it any way that you would like it to be.

Whatever process you used to bring these scenes to your mind is your way of "visualizing."

There are actually two different modes involved in creative visualization. One is the receptive, the other is active. In the receptive mode we simply relax and allow images or impressions to come to us without choosing the details of them; we take what comes. In the active mode we consciously choose and create what we wish to see or imagine. Both these processes are an important part of creative visualization, and your receptive and active abilities will both be strengthened through practice.

SPECIAL PROBLEMS WITH VISUALIZATION

Occasionally a person has completely blocked his ability to visualize or imagine at will, and feels that he simply "can't do it." This type of block usually arises from a fear, and it can be worked through if the person desires to do so.

Usually a person blocks his ability to use creative visualization out of a fear of what he may encounter by looking inside himself — fear of his own unacknowledged feelings and emotions.

For example, a man in one of my classes was consistently unable to visualize, and kept falling asleep during the meditations. It turned out that he had once had a profoundly emotional experience during a visualization process, and he was afraid he would be embarrassed by becoming emotional in front of others.

The truth is that there is nothing within us that can hurt us; it is only our fear of experiencing our own feelings that can keep us trapped.

If anything unusual or unexpected arises during meditation, the best thing is simply to look at it fully, be with it and experience it as much as you can, and you will find that it loses any negative power over you. Our fears arise from things we don't confront. Once we are willing to look fully and deeply at the source of a fear, it loses its power.

Fortunately, such problems with visualization are rare. As a rule, creative visualization comes naturally, and the more you practice it, the easier it will become.

BASIC STEPS FOR EFFECTIVE CREATIVE VISUALIZATION

Set Your Goal

Decide on something you would like to have, work toward, realize, or create. It can be on any level — job, a house, a relationship, a change in yourself, increased prosperity, a happier state of mind, improved health, beauty, or better physical condition, or whatever.

At first, choose goals that are fairly easy for you to believe in, that you feel are possible to realize in the fairly near future. That way you won't have to deal with too much negative resistance in yourself, and you can maximize your feelings of success as you are learning creative visualization. Later, when you have more practice, you can take on more difficult or challenging problems.

Create a Clear Idea or Picture

Create an idea or mental picture of the object or situation exactly as you want it. You should think of it in the present tense as already existing the way you want it to be. Picture yourself with the situation as you desire it, now. Include as many details as you can.

You may wish to make an actual physical picture of it as well, by making a treasure map (described in detail later). This is an optional step, not at all necessary, but often helpful (and fun!)

Focus on it Often

Bring your idea or mental picture to mind often, both in quiet mediation periods, and also casually throughout the day when you happen to think of it. In this way it becomes an integrated part of your life, it becomes more of a reality for you, and you project it more successfully.

Focus on it clearly, yet in a light, gentle way. It's important not to feel like you are striving too hard for it or putting an excessive amount of energy into it — that would tend to hinder rather than help.

Give it Positive Energy

As you focus on your goal, think about it in a positive, encouraging way. Make strong positive statements to yourself: that it exists, that it has come or is now coming to you. See yourself receiving or achieving it. These positive statements are called "affirmations." While you are using affirmations, try to temporarily suspend any doubts or disbelief you may have, at least for the moment, and practice getting the feeling that what you desire is very real and possible.

Continue to work with this process until you achieve your goal, or no longer have the desire to do so. Remember that goals often change before they are realized, which is a perfectly natural part of the human process of change and growth. So don't try to prolong it any longer than you have energy for it — if you lose interest it may mean that it's time for a new look at what you want.

If you find that a goal has changed for you, be sure to acknowledge that to yourself. Get clear in your mind about the fact that you are no longer focusing on your previous goal. End cycle on the old, and begin cycle on the new. This helps you avoid getting confused, or feeling like you've "failed" when you have simply changed.

When you achieve a goal, be sure to acknowledge consciously to yourself that it has been completed. Often we achieve things which we have been desiring and visualizing, and we forget to even notice that we have succeeded! So give yourself some appreciation and a pat on the back, and be sure to thank the universe for fulfilling your requests.

RELATED MEDITATIONS

Opening the Energy Centers

This is a meditation for healing and purifying your body, and for getting your energy flowing. It is an excellent one to do in the morning when you first wake up, or at the beginning of any meditation period, or anytime you want to be relaxed and refreshed:

Lie down on your back with arms at your sides or with hands clasped on your stomach. Close your eyes, relax and breathe gently, deeply and slowly.

Imagine that there is a glowing sphere of golden light surrounding the top of your head. Breathe deeply and slowly in and out five times while you keep your attention on the sphere of light, feeling it radiate from the top of your head.

Now allow your attention to move down to your throat. Again imagine a golden sphere of light emanating from your throat area. Breathe slowly in and out five times with your attention on this light.

Allow your attention to move down to the center of your chest. Once again imagine the golden light, radiating from the center of your chest. Again take five deep breaths, as you feel the energy expanding more and more.

Next put your attention on your solar plexus; visualize the sphere of golden light all around your midsection. Breathe into it slowly, five times.

Now visualize the light glowing in and around your pelvic area. Again take five deep breaths, feeling the light energy radiating and expanding.

Finally, visualize the glowing sphere of light around your feet, and breathe into it five more times.

Now imagine all six of the spheres of light glowing at once so that your body is like a strand of jewels, radiating energy.

Breathe deeply, and as you exhale, imagine energy flowing down along the outside of the left side of your body from the top of your head to your feet. As you inhale, imagine it flowing up along the right side of your body to the top of your head. Circulate it around your body this way three times.

Then visualize the flow of energy going from the top of your head down along the front of your body to your feet as you slowly exhale. As you inhale, feel it flow up along the back of your body to the top of your head. Circulate the flow in this direction three times.

Now imagine that the energy is gathering at your feet, and let it flow slowly up through the center of your body from your feet to your head, radiating from the top of your head like a fountain of light, then flowing back down the outside of your body to your feet. Repeat this several times, or as long as you wish.

When you finish this meditation you will be deeply relaxed, yet energized and exhilarated.

Pink Bubble Technique

This meditation is simple and wonderfully effective.

EXERCISE Sit or lie down comfortably, close your eyes and breathe deeply, slowly, and naturally. Gradually relax deeper and deeper.

Imagine something that you would like to manifest. Imagine that it has already happened. Picture it as clearly as possible in your mind.

Now in your mind's eye surround your fantasy with a pink bubble; put your goal inside the bubble. Pink is the color associated with the heart, and if this color vibration surrounds whatever you visualize, it will bring to you only that which is in perfect affinity with your being.

The third step is to let go of the bubble and imagine it floating off into the universe, still containing your vision. This symbolized that you are emotionally "letting go" of it. Now it is free to float around in the universe, attracting and gathering energy for its manifestation.

There is nothing more you need to do.

Contacting Your Inner Guide

Most of us in this day and age and in our Western society lead very hectic lives. We have many responsibilities: our work, our families, our friendships, our social, community, and political responsibilities. Even our recreational activities often take a lot of our attention and energy. We are very involved in what's outside us. Most of us are greatly in need of balancing this outward focus by taking some time to go within ourselves. We need to get back in contact with our spirit, with our inner creative source.

Change Occurs Naturally

If you feel your progress toward your goals is too slow, ask the universe for help. Remind yourself that things will always change in time. Change happens not by forcing it, but by becoming aware of what's not working in your life and being willing to let it go. Change, a dynamic, natural process, is always occurring, even when we're not aware of it.

I allow things to change in their own natural time.

I believe that each of us has a deep sense of truth within us, the guiding force that can lead us successfully through our lives. But when we spend most of our time looking outside ourselves, involved so intensely with the outside world, we lose contact with that spirit, with that creative source within us.

In addition, most of us have not been educated to believe in that inner intuitive knowingness. We've been taught to follow outside rules, other people's ideas of that's right and wrong for us or what we need to be doing. As a result, we lose touch with the very core of our being.

We need to take some time to cultivate contact with our inner guide. We need to reeducate ourselves to pay attention to that part of us that really knows. It helps if we can begin to take some regular time for this — even if it's just a few minutes each day or even a few minutes once a week. We need this time to learn to relax our bodies and our minds, to move into the deeper awareness that exists within us.

This takes practice, patience, and support. But it's something that's very natural for us, so as we begin to cultivate this habit we will find it easier and easier to go within. After a while we will begin to find that we crave this inner contact. When we spend too much time looking outward there will be a part of us that will start to pull us inside and demand that we get in contact with our deeper self.

Unblock the Flow

When we are blocking the flow of energy we begin to experience less and less vitality. As the flow diminishes, our bodies are slow to revitalize. They begin to age and deteriorate. Poor posture, tight jaws, headaches, and backaches are all reflections of chronic energy blocks.

By relaxing and nurturing ourselves, by healing our emotional wounds, by reaching for what gives us joy, we can release these patterns from our lives. In turn, our bodies will experience a new ease and new power.

I relax and nurture myself; I open to joy.

CHAPTER 8

Ohashiatsu® Touch

Ohashi

A native of Japan, Ohashi says his desire to help others started with the fact that he escaped three brushes with death before age three. The first was the bombing of Hiroshima, the second a case of malnutrition and the third, an accidental fall from a rooftop. These calamities left their mark on young Ohashi, but his strength was eventually restored by ancient Japanese healing methods. Because these techniques literally saved his life, Ohashi has dedicated himself to teaching these skills to others.

After graduation from Chuo University in Tokyo—where he studied American literature—Ohashi attended a school that specialized in shiatsu and other traditional healing modalities. It wasn't long before Ohashi was invited to New York to teach. He realized that many in the Western world were ready to accept the healing powers of the Orient, and he developed his own method—Ohashiatsu. More than just massage or physical manipulation, Ohashiatsu involves a caring exchange between giver and receiver to promote physical and psychological harmony within the individual.

Today, the non-profit Ohashi Institute in New York provides a meditative oasis for self-rejuvenation, to soothe the nervous system, to improve body awareness and for professional training; there are currently ten branch schools in the United States and Europe.

In addition to his work at the Ohashi Institute, and through lectures and workshops around the world, Ohashi has made his technique available for a broad audience through his many books and videotapes.

*I*n America's search for health and relief from tension "the natural way," more and more people have come across, or experienced, the Japanese art of *shiatsu*, sometimes called "acupuncture without needles." Ohashiatsu goes beyond traditional *shiatsu* by introducing psychological and spiritual components.

THE BALANCE OF NATURE

To understand Ohashiatsu, it is important to know something of the Oriental philosophy of the "balance of nature"—a viewpoint of life which teaches that the elements of nature work in harmony with each other and that we are a part of that relationship. All aspects of our lives are affected by these elements and the laws that govern them. The ancient Chinese established a highly refined society based on this philosophy, and developed effective healing modalities over thousands of years of experience.

The more our society places technology as the central focus of modern existence, the further away we drift from the essence of human nature. If we today are to be guided by the balance that exists in nature, we must recognize that nature has endowed us with the ability to acquire knowledge through the senses and intuition. These are important gifts that we can use to improve our health.

The basic virtue of sensing and intuiting is that they are nature's ways of instilling in us knowledge about ourselves and our relationship to the universe without conscious thought on the part of our intellect. Intuition and sensing are separate from intellect, but are meant to work in harmony with it.

KI ENERGY

Both acupuncture and Ohashiatsu follow the basic premise that the functioning of the human body is governed by what is called *ki* in Japanese. This invisible energy, defined in Western terms as an electromagnetic force, is a force that sustains and perpetuates life.

In the body, this energy travels along pathways which we call meridians. These 14 energy channels which flow through the body are composed of a series of points, or *tsubos*. By applying gentle pressure with the hands, elbows or thumbs to these points along the meridians, blocked energy is released and—since these energy channels connect with body organs--pressure applied to one part of the body can benefit another part. But Ohashiatsu is more than massage or touching. Its effectiveness also depends upon the flow of *ki* energy between the giver and the receiver.

In Oriental medicine and philosophy, a healthy life consists of *ki* energy. This *ki*-energy comes from two aspects—one is physical life and the other is spiritual and psychological life power. From birth to death, we are governed by this *ki*. Ancestral vitality comes from our parents as we are conceived and then born. The duration of life—from birth to death—is the duration of *ki*. When our *ki* fades out either physiologically or spiritually, our life returns to eternity. Here, "life" doesn't refer simply to the physiological body—bones, muscles, nails, hair. etc.—but also is part of that which is invisible, such as human spirit and emotions.

When we have a balance between the physical and the spiritual, then we have a joyful, stress-free life. In Ohashiatsu we deal with and balance these two aspects. By giving Ohashiatsu daily to your family or yourself, you can maintain this equilibrium, which tends to become distorted in our society due to environmental, social, political and economic reasons. Ohashiatsu allows our spirit to rise above this distortion and feel oneness with our bodies. When we feel oneness, there is life.

FOUR BASIC PHILOSOPHIES

Four basic philosophies form the foundation for Ohashiatsu. The first relates to the flow of *ki* energy between giver or receiver. Internally, each is sensing the other, forming a dependent, balanced relationship, where trust and complete relaxation can occur. (In fact, in many of the practices you will see in this chapter, both giver and receiver literally "support" one another—that is to say that one would fall over without the other.) This kind of internal activity—when the muscles are relaxed—is what we call "tonus."

A second principle of Ohashiatsu concerns the balance which is achieved when both hands work in harmony. As in the Oriental theory of yin and yang, neither can exist without the other. In Ohashiatsu, one hand is referred to as the

"Mother" hand; this hand remains stationary or supportive while the other, the "Son" hand, moves along the meridians, effecting changes. The Mother hand senses these changes as they occur. Any pain resulting from the Son hand along the meridian can be felt by the Mother hand, which balances out the Son hand, eliminating the pain. Thus, through the Mother hand we can diagnose the condition of the meridians, as well as balance them.

The third principle of Ohashiatsu is continuity. Like the dancer, the giver moves from one place on the body to another effortlessly, so that the receiver feels at one with the giver. This is very important, for it is through smooth and continuous movement that a feeling of trust develops between the receiver and the giver.

Finally, Ohashiatsu requires that we be natural. Part of being natural is knowing how to relax and flow with one's energy. In Ohashiatsu, we learn to remain calm and relaxed, even in activity. Being natural—when practicing Ohashiatsu—requires that both giver and receiver relax and open up to each other without pretense. Both must allow their bodies to remain in a state of "tonus."

Once you understand these four principles, Ohashiatsu is a simple method which can be learned by anyone, and may be practiced anytime, anywhere. It is a method that can be done with a partner or on oneself, with dramatic physical benefits. It can be used in longer, more thorough treatments, or just for a few minutes for general health or to relieve stress.

A full and healthy life, of course, does not necessarily begin and end on the physical level. With Ohashiatsu, learning and healing takes place not only with the body but also in the mind and spirit, for in the end it is the coordination and harmony of all three that expresses humanity.

Among the benefits of a regular practice of Ohashiatsu Touch techniques are:

- Greater sensitivity. Through Ohashiatsu, you become sensitive to your own imbalance of *ki* energy, as well as that of others. Your practice will cultivate your awareness of yourself—through touch, exercise and stretching. The

> "The future of touch is so immense. When I think about this subject, sometimes my body starts shaking. It is needed. In modern Western medicine, they don't touch our human body. My belief is that if we touch constantly, we can decrease our medical bill by half."
>
> —Ohashi, in an interview with *Massage* magazine

flow of *ki* energy between giver and receiver strengthens spirit, relieves tension, and therefore, promotes relaxation and vitality.

- A release of stagnant energy that causes pain or malaise. In Ohashiatsu, as we touch the body, we are manipulating the *ki* energy flow channels, called meridians. This releases stagnant energy by unblocking what we call "*tsubos*." We apply two hands to eliminate these stress-ridden *tsubos* through comfortable touch rather than painful application.

(*Note*: Effective Ohashiatsu should be a comfortable and meditative process; for this reason, Ohashiatsu should ideally be given when you are not distracted.)

- Positive and deep communication. Before verbal or intellectual communication, human touch was the first communication; touch is both basic and profound. In our high-tech world, we communicate by fax and computer. As society has developed technologically, people have drastically "lost touch." This dichotomy causes stress and tension because we need touch communication to connect with our life spirit.

Ohashiatsu, then, advances "touch-nology." It is high-touch for a high-tech world to transcend physical limitations in pursuit of relaxation and harmony.

How to Give Ohashiatsu to Others

The most significant characteristic of Ohashiatsu is how it develops and gives benefit to the giver. This is the basic difference between Ohashiatsu and other forms of bodywork. Giving and receiving Ohashiatsu creates a special relationship—both supportive and supporting. The giver does not suffer from giving. Instead, the giver enjoys sharing a relaxed state with the receiver. I, myself, feel more relaxed and rejuvenated after giving many treatments over the course of a day.

In giving Ohashiatsu to others, we must be relaxed for the receiver to get the full benefit. The more relaxed you are, the more relaxation you can provide for others. As giver, you don't need big muscles or unusual strength. The first lesson you learn in Ohashiatsu is that you don't press.

Just being together and supporting one another provides more than enough pressure. Pressure doesn't come from muscles or fingers, it flows from one's bodywieght.

It is important for the giver and the receiver to maintain good communication. The receiver should tell the giver how he or she feels and needs. Since everyone has a different sensitivity to touch, generalizations are less important than what giver and receiver can tell each other directly.

Prepare a comfortable environment to enjoy Ohashiatsu. Ideally, a quiet, relaxing and clean room with gentle music and incense is best. Use a mattress on the floor, or sit in a comfortable chair. Relax any tight-fitting clothes, such as ties, belts and remove shoes. If possible, remove all jewelry.

You don't need any special tools or equipment for Ohashiatsu. You can give it in a chair, on the floor, anytime, anywhere. These simple routines can create a harmonious lifestyle, achieve mutual happiness and provide maximum relaxation.

OHASHIATSU WITH A PARTNER

The following are exercises to be done with a partner. You may run through the entire sequence, or pick specific areas to work on.

It is important to keep in mind that one of the essentials of Ohashiatsu is you are not *doing* anything—you are just being there. Because of touching, being becomes doing—one supports the other. Both partners are completely relaxed. Each person must bring this concept to Ohashiatsu. Relax, trust and surrender.

SHOULDERS, NECK AND BACK   These next exercises may be done with the receiver seated comfortably on the floor, or on a chair. If receiver is sitting on the floor, stand or kneel behind her. If the receiver is sitting in a chair, stand behind her.

Place both hands on her shoulders. Apply your weight on her shoulders while remaining relaxed. Lean toward her, but do not press.

Slowly lean more, keeping palm on the shoulder, or using the thumb. You can lean with one leg down.

Wherever receiver feels most sensitive, remain in that area longer. (It is important for giver and receiver to communicate about this.)

You may also use your arm below the elbow to apply your body weight. Lean with your entire body, not just your elbow. Relax your fingers and just lean. The elbow goes up and down her neck and shoulder. Repeat this three times, changing the angle to accommodate receiver's needs and sensitivity.

After you finish this, you can put one hand on the shoulder and bring her left arm back. Stretch her left arm and apply elbow once more. Your elbow will be on her shoulder. Then lean toward her. When you lean, you move her arm and stretch it further. This is particularly effective for shoulder tension, headache.

After this, slowly apply your palm and thumb along her shoulder blade. Whether on floor or chair, apply left leg to support her left arm. Apply your left hand on the front of the shoulder. Bring her shoulder toward you. Place your right palm or thumb deep in, reach between the shoulder blade and spine. Bring her shoulder toward you and lean toward her. When you hit sensitive points, remain there and rotate thumb. Breath in and out together and remain completely relaxed.

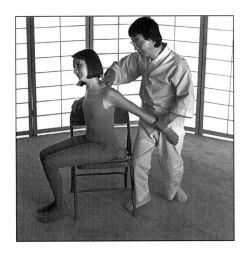

After you finish, apply your palms along the spine, and then apply thumbs to areas that are most sensitive. When you press her back, she may slide forward, so bring her shoulder back gently toward you. Your left knee should support her left arm.

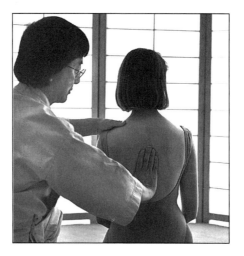

After you finish this, slide your palms down on either side of the spine seven times to release tension. Breathe together.

HEAD AND NECK   This is the most effective method for stress and tension and headaches. You can do this for five to ten minutes in the office, at home, on a train or plane. If you have only a few minutes with a partner, do this technique.

With your right hand, hold her temples. Your left hand is at the natural indentation at the back of the head. Apply your thumb and index finger to gently squeeze the neck. Your right hand squeezes the temple. Then rotate her neck as widely as possible by rotating your entire body. Her neck should rotate slowly, only as a result of your body rotating.

Bring her head back toward you. Lean back, so her chin goes up, and her head points up. Squeeze again with hands. Breathe together.

NECK STRETCHES Place your left hand under her head, just below the headbone, at the top of the neck. Put your fingers there. Your right hand should just rest on the eye socket, without pressing the eyes. Bring her head toward you—and just stay there.

This will help relieve headache, insomnia and chronic tension.

When you are holding her, put both hands on her neck. Pull her toward you and vibrate her head gently—this helps to release tension. She should exhale as you do this.

After this, put one thumb on the other thumb between her eyebrows. Press firmly—by leaning. When you apply your thumb, don't tense your thumb, just lean your body weight through your thumbs. This is very good for eye tension, eye stress.

After this, slowly pick up her head. Slide your right hand under her head into her left shoulder. Then stand your left leg up. Cradle her head. Then slowly lift her head toward the left side. Repeat this six or seven times. Don't move your hands; instead, raise your hips up. When she exhales, you lift her head as high as possible.

Then do the other side in reverse. This technique is especially good for a tired, aching neck.

After you finish both sides, then hold the head with your left palm. Squeeze the back of the neck with the right hand and lift her head. Lean toward her as you raise and stretch her neck.

This is a powerfully relaxing technique. Note that the receiver must completely relax her head, neck, finger and toes.

BACK RELAXERS   Receiver lies down on her stomach, with her arms up or down—whichever way is comfortable. Ideally, do this on the floor, on top of a folded blanket or futon.

Keeping arms straight but relaxed, lean your body weight. You may use your palm or thumb. If you are using your thumb with one hand, use your palm with the other. Use your entire body weight by moving, but do not press. Here, the receiver breathes out while you are leaning.

You may cross your hands, just as a pianist sometimes does, but continue resting your weight on straight and relaxed arms.

When you are using this technique, you relax and lean. Keep your spine straight and relaxed. Your thumb or palms run alongside the spine on either side, but not directly on the spine. Concentrate on areas where the receiver is most sensitive.

Next, you bend her legs and apply your weight on her back, not the legs. This will help relieve lower back strain and tightness from excessive sitting.

HOW TO GIVE OHASHIATSU TO YOURSELF

One of the advantages of self-Ohashiatsu is that you can give it to yourself anywhere in any form. Also, you are naturally already quite aware of your own physical needs, so you will know how deeply to touch and where to get the maximum results.

When you are giving Ohashiatsu to yourself, it is important to focus on your breathing. When you breathe out, you relax your muscles and energize your *ki*. This is when you can achieve the maximum benefit. In self-Ohashiatsu, we exhale, stretch, apply Ohashiatsu—hold for three to five seconds—and then move on to another point or stretch again.

Breathe slowly and deeply from your diaphragm. Nervous people tend to breathe shallowly from their chests and shoulders. Diaphragmatic breathing provides more relaxed breathing than chest breathing.

Don't tense any part of the body. Just lean and move—use your own body weight and energy. Keep your body loose all the time. Shift your weight, but do not push. When you give Ohashiatsu to yourself, you are both giver and receiver. You are communicating with yourself on a subtle, but deep level within a highly meditative state. *Ki* energy flows through you, as electricity would through a closed circuit—an unbroken flow of energy.

Hara Breathing

Hara is the area of the body between the solar plexus and the pelvic bone. To the Japanese, *hara* is considered the center of our being, our vitality. To develop the *hara* is to develop vitality and dignity. In Ohashiatsu, all our activity and energy flow begins at the *hara*—with the breath.

Sit down comfortably, whether you cross your legs on the floor or sit in a chair. Apply both hands (palms down) to your *hara*.

Breathe in and breathe out—when you breathe out, put your fingers from both hands deep and hold then move your fingers clockwise.

Repeat this three times.

When you are breathing out, bend out and move your fingers clockwise. Do this technique all over the belly.

(The reason we do this in a clockwise motion is that the intestine runs in a clockwise motion. This way, you relax your internal organs and you control your breathing. When you control your breathing, you relax your emotional state. I highly recommend you do this in the morning, evening, or whenever you can—on an airplane or bus—as a discrete but wonderful way to relax from your daily tensions. It can also make your digestive system stronger.)

Tension Release Exercise

This is an exercise to release tension in the extremities. All our energy stagnates at extremities such as toes, fingers. For example, when we are nervous or upset, our face may be smiling diplomatically, but our toes or fingers are tight. Our real emotions flow to our extremities.

To release tension, you interlock your fingers and turn hands inside out. When you are breathing in, you bend your elbows and bring your hands toward your chest.

When you breathe out, stretch all the way. Then you feel the relaxation from the back of the chest all the way to the finger-tips. Ideally, you can shout, chant or make some noise while you stretch and exhale.

Repeat this seven times. Each time, breathe in slowly, imagine that you are bringing all the available air into your entire body. When you are breathing out, breathe as if you are squeezing all the air from your fingertips and toetips, head, spine—exhale completely, drain out. Hold as long as possible and then breathe in slowly. Each segment (in/out) should take about seven seconds. The more slowly you do this, the more you benefit.

This technique is very good for anxiety and stress.

ARMS   After you stretch, you can begin work on your arms.

Here, we follow the meridians: along the outside of the arm (the yang), and the inside (the yin).

Beginning with the yang, start with fingertips. Hold arms out, elbows bent, with fingers of both hands touching. Hold the right hand with the left hand. Apply your left hand to press between the index finger and thumb. This is a very sensitive point. This is very good for tension in the face. Press with a rotating motion. I can recommend this for a toothache and tight jaw.

Now, slowly go up to the elbow pressing with the thumb. Just below the elbow is a very sensitive point. You can apply a good deal of pressure here; when you hit the right point, you feel a slight shock. This is good for tired arms and tension in the shoulder. I highly recommend this for people who type or use computers all day.

Then, turn palms upside-down. Find the center of your palm—the deepest indentation. Press very hard toward your elbow. This is a good point for anxiety, nervousness, impatience—an effective way to calm down. Press towards the elbow—sometimes I use my fist or elbow. Do whatever feels natural. (Banging this point with fist is an instinctive human behavior.)

Move your fingers up, and when you are touching the center of the arm, find the most sensitive point and hold it. Then rotate you thumb and at the same time rotate your right hand—coordinate these movements. Press deeply. Breathe out, chant, sing—imagine you are in beautiful surroundings, breathing clean air.

After you've finished the inside and outside of the arms, then pull your fingertips all the way—you keep squeezing—hold it, shake it and then snap it.

If your knuckles crack, do not be disturbed; it is just your joints loosening up.

LEGS   Whether exercising, walking slowly, standing or sitting, your legs will at some point experience fatigue, and in need of attention. These exercises will release stagnant *ki* energy to rejuvenate and relax.

To begin, focus on the inside of your legs.

Stretch your right leg and bend your left leg. Squeeze the big toe. Press hard and rotate the very sensitive point between the big toe and second toe with your fingers as you breathe out.

Go up the leg, press and rotate on the ankle joint. Slowly stretch leg out. Put your palm along shinbone outside. This is good for tired legs. Rotate your thumb and squeeze your leg. You'll feel a strong sensation. Adjust your fingers to touch wherever you are most sensitive. It is quite normal to feel a little pain, when you do this—be sure to focus on your breathing.

Now, bend your right leg around in front of you, with the sole of your right foot facing up. Place your left elbow on the soft indented (concave) part of the sole; when you are breathing out, lean into your foot. This is an energy center—a point of vitality. When you feel drained, working this point will be helpful. Don't be afraid to dig in with your elbow. This movement is also good for your lower back.

Starting from the foot, move your elbow up to lower leg and then upper leg. Always lean over and apply weight when you are exhaling. Don't press with your arm or elbow—just lean and use the weight of your body.

Repeat these exercises—three times for each leg, before moving to outside of legs.

Now you can begin to work the outside of your legs. Whereas on the inside of our legs we worked from the foot up to the hip, here we move in the opposite direction.

First, open your fingers, put your elbow on the hip socket and work down to your feet (three or five points along the way). Just search for the points that give you the strongest sensations. This is very effective for tired legs, general fatigue and poor circulation.

If you are doing vigorous exercise, it is a good idea to do these leg exercises as both a warm-up and a cool-down.

After you finish inside and outside of both legs, bend both legs up, knees out. Bring your feet as close as possible to your body. Slowly bend forward on the exhale. Do this seven times.

Remember never to force yourself—-just let your body go; this way you are releasing tension without a struggle.

FACE, HEAD AND NECK   The face is the area in which we accumulate our tension most of all, due to eye fatigue, sinuses, headaches, and tightly clenched jaws. The lines on the accompanying photos illustrate the direction and approximate locations you should place your hands when touching the face.

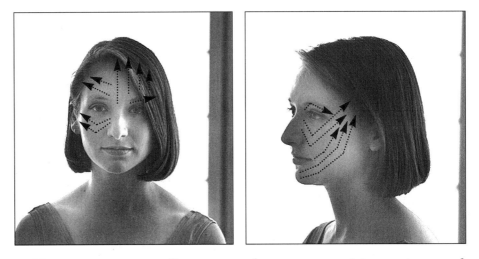

You can put your fingers on the most sensitive points and rotate clockwise. Breathe in and then out. Make some noise. Release tension. Chant or sing or shout. Some of these points are very sensitive. Stay longer on these points until pain decreases. When you are holding these points, move your mouth—smile, frown, make expressions.

After this, place your hands on your temples and squeeze inside. This is particularly effective for headaches or anxiety. Place your thumb just behind the eyes and squeeze. Open your fingers and move them.

Now, place your hands on the top of the head, with fingers pointing in. Press hard and rotate your fingers. This will relax your nervous system, and help clear your thoughts. Use four fingers of each hand.

Now, move your left hand to the temple. Put the right thumb just below the head, at the top of the neck. Bring your head towards the right thumb and press hard against the thumb. This will help to relieve anxiety, insomnia and sinus problems. Then lean slightly backwards. This is a very powerful relaxer.

After this, you bend your head down. Interlock your fingers around the back of your neck. Squeeze your neck with your hands, beginning from your elbows. Your elbow should be rotating and moving. Bend your head down, relax, use your elbows to rotate. Go from the top of your head all the way down to your shoulders.

You can do these face, head and neck exercises in the office, on an airplane, whenever you feel tense and need relief. When you are suffering from a bad headache, or have just experienced a particularly stressful situation, these head and neck techniques (especially when combined with arm and finger exercises) can be very effective in relieving pain.

CHAPTER 9

Conscious Exercise

Dan Millman

A former world champion athlete who was recently voted into the Gymnastics Hall of Fame, author Dan Millman has generated an approach to living he calls "the way of the peaceful warrior"—the title Millman gave his first book. That book sold over one million copies and today his books have been read by more than two million people, fourteen languages worldwide.

Millman has served on the faculties at Oberlin College, the University of California at Berkeley and Stanford University. For the past decade, he has trained people from all walks of life including physicians, therapists, educators and others involved in the fields of personal and spiritual growth. Currently, Dan lives in northern California; his lectures and training sessions take him around the world.

Several years ago, a high school student approached me and said, "I need some professional advice but don't have much money, so I'd like to buy a dollar's worth of your time. What can you tell me in thirty seconds?"

I considered this for about twenty-eight seconds; then I gave him advice that could change the quality of his life: "Breathe and relax."

Even if he had paid me ten thousand dollars, that young man had just received the best bargain of his life ~ or he had wasted his time and his money ~ depending entirely upon what he did with that bit of guidance.

I open this chapter with the reminder that the "secrets" of relaxation (or anything else) tend to remain secret; not because so few of us know about them, but because so few of us actually practice them. Without practice, we only collect data, store it on a notepad, audiotape, or in our head. But only when we take what we know out of the files and apply it in daily life can it make a difference. The moment we turn understanding into action, magic happens.

Even small changes can make a very big difference, because simplicity has power; even a little can go a long way. My two-second's worth of advice (to breathe and relax) illustrates what I call the minimalist school of transformation. Such a "lazy" approach has great efficiency and power, as any martial arts master will tell you. The minimalist asks, "Why exert more effort than I need to accomplish my goal?" Whether your goal is finishing school, making more money or walking across the room, excess effort is wasteful. Most of us appreciate that a relaxed approach to life has a certain grace, elegance and style. But, given the stresses of daily life, relaxing isn't always easy to do.

This chapter highlights the full potential and promise of dynamic relaxation in creating a healthier, happier quality of life. Let's start with a look at how relaxation is key to optimal fitness.

MODELS OF FITNESS

Our concepts of fitness have changed over the years. Survival of the fittest used to mean survival of the strongest, the toughest. So those of us with the biggest muscles were viewed as the most fit; and since most men had larger muscles than women, they appeared to be more fit. Then someone noticed that large muscles didn't guarantee longevity or prevent heart attacks. So we looked deeper into the body for the answers.

Aerobics, first popularized by Dr. Kenneth Cooper, redefined fitness as a strong cardio-vascular system ~ a healthy heart, lungs, and capillaries. But our understanding of fitness continues to grow as we look still deeper into the body.

I suggest that we are in the process of another paradigm shift, and will soon redefine fitness in terms of neuromuscular health, or a general state of emotional equanimity, inner peace, and physical relaxation ~ what ancient healers, yogis, and martial arts masters have known for centuries ~ that a relaxed body, relatively free from the burdens of mental stress and emotional turmoil, enjoys good vital energy and a strong immune system. So relaxation isn't just a desirable frill at the edge of our lives; it may be a key to our full potential.

DYNAMIC RELAXATION

We normally associate relaxation with stillness, as in sleep, trance, or meditation. But life isn't lived in a sitting position. The highest form of relaxation is dynamic. The ancient martial artists, living and moving in the moment of truth, had to relax or die. Tension was fatal because it slowed reflexes; so just when the pressure was strongest, in crisis moments, the warriors learned to let go of attachments or expectations and to relax into life or into death. This was the highest practice and also the most difficult.

The cat, the ultimate warrior, is a supreme model of relaxation-in-action. In one moment, it moves with lightning reflexes to catch a flying insect or to repel a curious dog; in the next moment, it sits purring, licking its paws. To move like a cat is to master the art of dynamic relaxation ~ accomplishment with a sense of ease.

I suggest that we are in the process of another paradigm shift, and will soon redefine fitness in terms of neuromuscular health, or a general state of emotional equanimity, inner peace, and physical relaxation.

The less effort,
the faster and
more powerful
you will be.

-Bruce Lee

The benefits of practicing dynamic relaxation include:

- increased available energy

- less fatigue

- more stamina and endurance

- increased coordination

- improved balance, reflex speed

- better sense of timing and rhythm

- a more youthful, supple, elastic body

DYNAMIC RELAXATION AS A KEY TO NATURAL TALENT

To really appreciate the power of dynamic relaxation, let's explore the concept of natural talent.

When we say that someone is a "natural," we usually mean that they have innate talent in a given area. But we all have innate potential, and as it turns out, the more relaxed we become, the more we raise our level of "natural talent."

In my own training and research over the years, I found four primary qualities that make up physical talent. By developing all four qualities, we increase our potential in sports, games, martial arts, music, dance, or any other form of skill training. I call these qualities the Four S's of physical talent. They include:

When you
cannot see
what is
happening
do not stare
harder.
Relax and
look gently
with your
inner eye.

-Lao Tsu

1 *Strength*, or muscular control ~ the ability to move effectively even against resistance in the field of gravity.

2 *Suppleness*, flexibility, elasticity, or optimal range of motion, as desired or needed for specific skills.

3 *Stamina*, or endurance, means the ability to persist over time in a particular endeavor or form of training.

4 *Sensitivity* is composed of varied qualities, including balance, rhythm, timing, reflex speed, and coordination.

A key point in this chapter is that our ability to relax enhances all four S's of talent; the more you can relax while moving, the more effective your strength, suppleness, stamina, and sensitivity.

I think you can appreciate how relaxing can improve suppleness, because it's easier to develop and maintain flexibility in relaxed muscles. It also stands to reason that relaxed movement increases stamina because we can perform longer without getting tired. You also understand how a relaxed body has greater sensitivity ~ coordination, reflex speed, timing, and balance.

But how can relaxing possibly make us stronger? Don't muscles have to contract, or tense, in order to generate movement? Of course they do; but relaxed muscles generate more effective strength with less effort than chronically tense muscles. You can experience this yourself by doing the following exercise drawn from the martial art of Aikido:

THE UNBENDABLE ARM— A PARTNER EXERCISE

EXERCISE Hold your arm out in front of you, slightly bent, with your elbow pointing toward the ground, your fist clenched, and your wrist resting on your partner's shoulder. Your partner will place a hand on top of that arm, at the crook of the elbow, and gradually begin to push downward in order to bend your arm. Tense your arm; use strength to resist your partner, who continues pushing until the arm bends or you both get tired.

The same exercise as Part 1, with two important changes:

EXERCISE First, instead of clenching your fist, open your hand and fingers wide; second, instead of tensing your arm to resist your partner's push, keep your arm and shoulder relaxed. Instead of using strength, imagine that your arm is like a fire hose with water running more and more rapidly through it, so that the more

In Judo, he who thinks is immediately thrown. Victory is assured to those who are physically and mentally non-resistant.

-Robert Linssen

your partner pushes to bend your arm, the fast the water rushes through your arm and out your fingertips, making the arm long, extended, and very difficult to bend (much like a fire hose when water is surging through it).

Please note that it doesn't matter whether or not your partner can bend your arm; the point is to let you and your partner feel the difference between strength based on tension, and strength based upon "energy flow" (relaxation), in which you use only the muscles you need, and only to the extent you need them. The results can be dramatic.

If you don't have a partner handy, you can also experience the power of dynamic relaxation to increase effective strength by jumping into the air two times. The first time you jump, bend your knees, tense all your muscles, then jump. The second time you jump, stay relaxed as you bend your knees, then jump. Feel the difference. Or try doing two push ups, one tense all the way through, and one while remaining consciously relaxed.

FROM "TRYING" TO "LETTING"

One way to understand and apply a relaxed attitude toward sports and life is by shifting your emphasis from trying to letting. For example, most golfers understand the importance of letting the weight of the clubhead swing through the ball rather than trying to hit it. It's true in any form of movement, on the field or in daily life. When we try it implies that we might not be up to a task; it implies doubt, effort, even straining, all of which create counterproductive tension. In my book, *The Inner Athlete*, I point out that if someone asked you to get them a glass of water, you probably wouldn't answer, "I'll try." If you did try, you might very well trip on a chair, drop the glass, and fall out the kitchen window.

By letting things happen, you tend to move more easily and efficiently, using only those muscles you need in a relaxed, natural way. So let yourself hit the ball, open the car door, make the speech, ask for a date, or meet a deadline, and notice how life starts feeling easier.

CONSCIOUS EXERCISE

Once you understand the Four S's that make up physical talent, you're ready to fully appreciate the concept of conscious exercise, how it centers around dynamic relaxation, and how it can make a difference in our lives.

We exercise all the time, but not in any conscious way. Any time we move our bodies ~ whether playing a sport or game or just walking across a room ~ we exercise muscles, heart, and lungs. Conscious exercise, in contrast, involves repeated practice, over time, with gradually increasing demand or overload leading to refined or increased capacity. The kinds of conscious exercise we do depend upon the results we want. We may practice meditation exercises, strength exercises, stretching exercises, relaxation exercises, or all of these to reach specific, desired goals.

We pursue popular sports, games, and pastimes such as tennis, golf, racquetball, and bowling as diversion, entertainment, and recreation. In other words, bowlers, golfers, tennis and racquetball players, and others play because they like the game, not because they seek a total fitness routine. That they get some exercise is a plus, but not their first priority.

Unlike most sports and games, conscious exercise is specifically designed for the overall well-being of the body, mind, and emotions. A complete and efficient routine of conscious exercise usually has the following qualities:

- It develops all four S's of physical talent ~ strength, suppleness, stamina, and sensitivity

- It energizes rather than fatigues

- It creates symmetry (balances both sides of the body)

One of the key benefits of conscious exercise is that after we rhythmically and actively tense muscles, we feel a resulting sense of relaxation, ease, and tension release. From this observation, we can also derive a key principle: conscious tension releases chronic tension. Those of us who do not engage some active form of physical exercise, whether walking, swimming, sports or games, may and often do develop unconscious holding patterns of chronic tension in neck, shoulders, upper and lower back, abdomen, buttocks, or thighs. By moving these areas, through conscious tension we call exercise, we release the chronic tension. That's one primary reason that we feel so good after exercise.

Conscious exercise, then, is designed to help us feel more relaxed, and at the same time, more energized, after we finish than before we started.

Ancient sages, monks, dancers, and martial artists from various cultures of India and China created different forms of conscious exercise, including hatha yoga, T'ai Chi, and Chi Kung, and dance forms aimed at quieting the mind and balancing the body, generating healing, longevity, equanimity, and serenity. Modern forms of conscious exercise include systems such as Arica Psychocalisthenics™, swimming, basic gymnastics, and certain non-impact aerobics disciplines. Common to all forms of conscious exercise is the importance of dynamic relaxation.

In 1985, I developed an efficient routine of conscious exercise for busy modern men and women ~ *The Peaceful Warrior Workout* ™ video ~ a unique, four-minute routine of movement, deep breathing, and tension release. This flowing routine is designed to integrate body, mind, and emotions. It is composed of 15 movements, blending elements of strength, suppleness, stamina, and sensitivity.

FREE MOVEMENT

One of the key exercises from the peaceful warrior workout is called free movement. In infancy, you practiced free movement most of the day as you explored your growing ability to move in every conceivable direction; you learned to stretch, crawl, roll, turn, and twist. In one physical education research study, a number of college athletes attempted to keep up with active one-year olds, duplicating their movements. Within a few minutes, the athletes gave up, exhausted.

After infancy, your freedom of movement and expression probably became more structured. Most of us have settled into familiar patterns of movement: We stand, sit, drive, eat, type, write, soap off in the shower, brush our teeth, and often make love in the same familiar patterns, so that our movements are neither truly "free" nor relaxed ~ almost as if the body doesn't feel safe exploring new territory.

The danger here is that by restricting the body to rigid or set patterns, the brain also forms rigid or structured, non-creative ways of thinking. Over time, we may succumb to a condition of "psycho-sclerosis" (hardening of the attitudes).

By consciously exploring random, flowing, continuous, instinctive, spontaneous, uninhibited, even "mindless" movement, we stimulate the entire neuromuscular system, and reactivate our physical and mental creative capacities, opening new ways to think and move.

EXERCISE We multiply the benefit of free movement many times over by paying attention to the following principles while moving:

1 Move in a flowing, continuous manner;

2 Explore movements near the floor as well as tall, light, or expansive movements while standing;

3 Breathe profoundly and deeply, letting the breath flow with, or even initiate the movements;

4 Stay as relaxed as possible, feeling that the movements happen almost by themselves.

Now, or at your next opportunity, take one to three minutes to practice free movement, either to music, or in silence, as you prefer. You may be pleasantly surprised to realize what a good workout you get in a very short time.

Such an expression of dynamic relaxation doesn't just feel good; it gets results.

SLOW MOTION

Legend has it that a certain master of T'ai Chi Ch'uan, the slow-moving, dance-like Chinese martial art, was so relaxed and sensitive that if a fly landed on him, his whole body would sway. It is said that this master could hold a wild sparrow captive in his open palm; birds have to push off with their legs before their flapping wings take them aloft, and each time the sparrow's feet pushed, the master's hand would give way like air, epitomizing, like the cat, mastery of the art of relaxation in action.

Many of us who have seen or practiced T'ai Chi begin to appreciate slow motion is the most powerful method available to develop dynamic relaxation. Performing any movement very slowly enables us to notice and release any tension that might have otherwise gone unnoticed and unresolved. The following exercise helps to illustrate this important principle:

EXERCISE Hold your palm up in front of you, about a foot from your face. Now, in one quick movement, turn your palm away from you as you extend your entire arm out to the side of your body.

Notice how you were aware of your arm while you were looking at your palm, before you moved it, and again after you moved it. But how much awareness did you have while you were moving it?

EXERCISE Repeat the same set-up and movement as before, starting with your palm in front of you; but this time, move in very slow motion as you slowly turn your palm away and extend your arm to the side. Move as slowly as the shifting of a sand dune, or a pebble sinking down through thick honey. And as you move, ask yourself, Is my shoulder relaxed as I move? Are my arm and hand relaxed? Am I moving only my arm, or am I turning my body as well? How would it feel if I also turned my body? Is the rest of my body relaxed? Am I breathing slowly and deeply? How would it feel to coordinate my breathing with my movement, to exhale as I move? You could ask yourself other questions, too, because you have the time to do so; you have time to become aware.

Moving in slow motion can be difficult or frustrating, even "maddening" for some of us used to moving quickly, because when we move slowly, we become aware of the tension we carry and have the opportunity to release it.

EXERCISE Go through another movement you do at home or in your favorite pastime, such as a golf swing, a tennis serve, throwing a ball, shooting a basket, doing a dance movement, or even bringing an imaginary fork from the plate to your mouth, but move in extreme slow motion.

Students of any martial art, sport, or game can benefit immensely from slow-motion practice as a means to master the art of dynamic relaxation.

DYNAMIC RELAXATION AND EMOTIONAL TENSION

Athletes and others involved in exercise and sports sometimes let frustration get the better of them. Have you noticed that when you feel angry your body tenses? Even more interesting, when your body relaxes, it is very difficult to feel as angry ~ at least experience it with the same intensity. As you relax and breathe, the contraction dissolves.

That isn't to say anger or any other emotion is bad or wrong or that we shouldn't feel it; on the contrary, emotions pass over us like waves or changing weather ~ but when we are able to stay physically relaxed and emotionally open, we let the feelings flow through us rather than inhibiting our movement or expression. Relaxation short-circuits the harmful effects of emotional tension, allowing the flow of energy to remain unobstructed so that we continue to act and move effectively.

Emotional tension develops as mental structures ~ attitudes, expectations, hopes, desires, wishes, wants, and values ~ conflict with or resist what happens in our lives, moment to moment. In other words, mental resistance or internal conflict (stress) imposes tension on the body.

Wilhelm Reich said, "Unexpressed emotions are stored in the muscles as physical tension"; that's the main reason most of us become less flexible over time. The years don't do it to us; we do it to ourselves over the years.

Young children are physically relaxed because they are also emotionally open, letting feelings flow then letting them go. But as we grow older and develop expectations, rigid beliefs, shame, guilt, and other mental structures, our free emotional expression becomes inhibited. By ten years old, most children first begin to complain of muscular soreness and tension—stiff necks, pulled muscles, lack of flexibility. By the time most of us have reached adulthood, we have developed numerous chronic holding patterns. This following simple diagnostic test can help you become more aware of the tension you hold in your upper arms, shoulders, upper back, and neck:

EXERCISE Standing still, turn your hips and waist left then right. Keep your arms, shoulders, neck, and back as relaxed as you can, so that your arms just flop and swing in response to the movement of your hips. In other words, imagine your arms and shoulders are like wet noodles, just hanging there, with no muscles.

Once your arms and shoulders feel relaxed and loose, have a partner play with one of your arms at a time, lifting it, letting it go, shaking it, turning and moving it throughout its natural range of motion (being careful not to twist or strain it).

Notice whether you unconsciously "help" your partner to lift your arm; notice whether it drops quickly and completely when released. Notice if you exert muscular tension or effort at any time, or whether your arms remain completely relaxed.

This exercise is not a "pass or fail" test; it is just one way of becoming aware of tension. Remember this principle: Awareness of tension is the beginning of relaxation. Until you notice the tension you carry, it is virtually impossible to let it go.

Another principle: As your awareness of tension expands, you will feel like you're getting more tense. I experienced this principle when I first began to practice the martial art of Aikido, which requires and develops a kind of relaxed strength based on "energy flow" rather than muscular tension. I had practiced gymnastics for years, and depended on my physical strength. So when I practiced responding to an attack, I tended to use my strength. My instructor kept reminding me, "Relax, relax…" but I didn't understand at first. I was trying like hell to relax! I soon started to feel like I was more tense than I had ever been before. In fact, I was not more tense; I was only becoming aware of how tense I had always been. Just when I seemed to be getting worse, as this awareness-of-tension grew, I began to let it go. A third principle: Awareness heals.

If I advise someone to "relax" when they are sitting in a chair, lying down to go to sleep, making love or practicing a golf swing, my advice may not be effective if they aren't aware of what "relaxation" really feels like, or if they believe they are already relaxed. Therefore, each of us needs to have a direct experience of what our body and mind feel like when we are deeply relaxed. We can find such direct experience through meditation practice, relaxation exercises, massage, or other methods outlined in this book. However you access that state, each time your body relaxes consciously (in contrast to unconsciously, as in deep sleep,) you can return to that state more easily, at will, even in moments you might otherwise become tense. And the more your body learns to relax, the less tolerant it becomes of chronic tension; you notice tension more quickly and easily, and can do whatever you need to let it go and return to a natural, youthful state of ease, equanimity, and grace.

EURYTHMICS AND AWARENESS

One useful exercise to increase our awareness of tension and our ability to relax comes from the practice of eurythmics, which means "good rhythm." The following exercise increases your capacity to consciously tense or release at will.

EXERCISE Using a metronome, ticking clock, or just by counting to yourself, through the following progressive steps:

1 Inhale to a count of six (about one count each second);

2 Hold the breath for a count of one;

3 Exhale to a count of six;

4 Pause for a count of one.

After that rhythm of breathing to a six count inhale, hold, six count exhale, and pause is comfortable, add the next step:

As you inhale, gradually tense every muscle in your body, so that at one you have little tension, at two, more… and at the count of six your entire body is very tense.

Then hold the tension for one count as you hold your breath.

Then, as you begin to exhale, let the muscles gradually relax, back to a count of one.

Completely relax as you pause for a count of one.

Then continue the inhale-tension process, hold, and exhale-relax, pause.

Over time, you can develop the ability to do this tension and relaxation cycle with the breathing on specific muscle groups, such as just the arms (biceps), or just the legs (bending and tensing), or a combination of different muscles. Over time, this ability to tighten some muscle groups while keeping others completely relaxed sends a flash of awareness and conscious control throughout your body. When you can consciously tense, you can consciously relax.

Be aware that the degree to which you will actually allow yourself to benefit from what you learn in this book ~ the degree to which you are willing to make your life easier by practicing dynamic relaxation and conscious exercise ~ depends primarily on your level of self-worth and trust. Only when you feel you deserve a life of relative ease ~ only when you come to fully trust the process of your life ~ will you allow yourself to let go, take a deep breath and relax into life. Those of us who operate on the belief that we have to suffer and sweat and strain for everything we get (because we don't feel

DAN MILLMAN

we deserve to have it easy), unconsciously create difficulties. I suggest you stick a note up on your bathroom mirror or somewhere else you'll see it every morning: "How easy can I stand it today?"

That's how easy you'll get it.

THE WAY OF THE PEACEFUL WARRIOR

As you become aware of tension as it arises in the course of our daily lives, sometimes through symptoms of discomfort, you begin the rejuvenating process of returning to physical birthright ~ a natural state of ease.

Late one night in a gas station, the old man I called Socrates reminded me, "Musicians practice music; poets practice poetry; the peaceful warrior practices everything, and that makes all the difference."

"How do you do that?" I asked.

"When you can treat opening a door, taking a bite of food, or walking across a room with the same attention and grace you bring to your golf swing, or a double somersault, or your backhand, you'll be practicing. Life is the practice arena; every movement you make becomes your game. In any moment, ask yourself three questions: 'Am I relaxed?' 'Am I breathing easily?' 'Am I moving with attention and refinement?' Then you are practicing life; then life gets very interesting, because no matter what else you are doing, you're always practicing. As your practice gets better, so does your life."

By incorporating dynamic relaxation into our chosen form of skill training, and more importantly, into our daily lives, we turn what we know into what we actually do; we finally lose our minds and come to our senses. By making dynamic relaxation your moment-to-moment practice, you improve the quality of your life.

RELAXATION PRACTICE

Even if you have done relaxation exercises before, you might want to have a friend read you the following script, or record it and play it back for yourself as you go through the following deep relaxation experience in which we use the image of heaviness to induce a deep state of relaxation as the body releases its holding patterns and remembers.

EXERCISE Lie comfortably on your back. If you wish, put pillows under your knees, arms, and head; whatever helps you lie comfortably.

Become aware of your body pressing down into the bed or floor, and the bed or floor pushing equally back against your body, supporting it.

Feel a pleasant sense of heaviness, as if your skin is heavy, your bones are heavy; feel the whole body as heavy. Let go of thoughts about whether you are doing it well enough or correctly, and just feel a sense of heaviness.

Gradually, at your own pace, feel a profound sense of heaviness and ease pervade your feet and ankles... skin heavy, bones heavy, and the whole body, heavy...

Now feel that heaviness pass up through your lower legs, shins, calves, up through the knees... skin, bones, the whole body...

Feel the heaviness pass up through your upper legs, your thighs, so that your entire legs are heavy...

Feel the heaviness pass up through your buttocks, pelvis, and lower abdomen, so breathing rises and falls of its own accord, effortlessly...

Feel the heaviness pass up the spine and back, under the shoulder blades, and up the abdomen and chest, spreading into the shoulders... skin heavy, bones heavy, and the whole body, heavy...

Let the heaviness pass into the upper arms, the elbows, and the forearms, right out to the palms and fingers, to the tips, so that your entire body below the neck is heavy... skin, bones, the whole body, heavy...

If you become aware of even the slightest holding or tension, let it go, let it sink down with gravity, becoming twice as heavy...

Feel the heaviness release the muscles of the neck, in front, the sides, the back... skin, bones, the whole body...

Feel the face as heavy, releasing, sinking down, the scalp, the ears...the forehead... the eyes and eyebrows... the cheeks... the mouth, and chin, and jaw... so that the skin is heavy, the bones are heavy, the whole body is heavy...

Now begin to feel the body as so light, transparent, that it can float easily, effortlessly, on your own private ocean... the water is warm as you float on your back, rising as if on a gentle swell as you inhale, and as you exhale, feel yourself float gently down, growing even more relaxed...

Now imagine yourself lying on a soft blanket, in warm sand at a quiet beach... perhaps you hear the sounds of waves or wind, or the cry of gulls in the distance...

You feel so relaxed, at ease, imagine that you sit up, effortlessly, using only the muscles you need, nothing more, as you stand, and walk, striding gracefully, elegantly... and this feels so good you run, loping along with such ease that you could run forever.

Now imagine yourself practicing or playing a game, sport, or movement art with the same effortless quality of ease and dynamic relaxation. How good can you feel? How little energy can you use and still move with efficiency?

Let your body remember this ease, and when you return to normal consciousness, let it adapt more and more to such ease, this state of dynamic relaxation...

Now, when ready, take three deep breaths, each breath deeper than the last, and with a third deep breath, feeling refreshed, awake, alive, and relaxed, stretch like a cat, and sit or stand, remembering how relaxed you can feel in stillness or in motion.

DAN MILLMAN

CHAPTER 10

New Technologies

Michael Hutchison
& Terry Patten

For over a decade, "high-tech guru" Michael Hutchison's explorations of the technology of peak performance have defined "the cutting edge." In his landmark work, *Megabrain,* Hutchison explored in depth a variety of techniques used to alter brainwave activity.

Hutchison's writings explore a broad spectrum of interplay between science and culture and information and power. His published works include: *The Book of Floating, Megabrain,* and most recently, *The Anatomy of Sex and Power: An Investigation of Mind-Body Politics.* His fiction has been awarded the James Michener Prize; his non-fiction has appeared in *Esquire, The Village Voice, Partisan Review* and *Playboy,* among other magazines and newspapers.

Terry Patten and his wife Leslie, founded Tools for Exploration in 1988 as a manufacturing and sales organization for BioCircuit ™ products. Tools for Exploration has quickly grown into a $2 million-a-year corporation dedicated to bringing the latest and best innovations to a broad audience, and developing the market for these products as well.

Patten has written on, lectured and taught meditation and spiritual systems through The Laughing Man Institute. He has lectured and led workshops on biocircuitry, consciousness technologies, bioelectricity and subtle energy flows. He is Founder and Director of Neuro-Acoustic Laboratories, author of *BioCircuits: Amazing New Tools for Energy Health,* and serves as managing Editor of *Megabrain Report: The Consciousness Technology Newsletter.*

Lying on her back, lightly grasping two copper handles, she exhaled deeply, obeying the instructions to "let go completely." At first, she noticed nothing special, just the sounds in the room around her and the weight of her body pressing against the couch.

Suddenly she felt a dramatic wave of relaxation, reminiscent of the rushing descent people feel when an airplane abruptly loses altitude. The cells of her body seemed to yawn open into a slumberous field of bliss. She imagined a rich liquid sensuously enveloping her body.

As she floated in this pleasurable state, the sensations gradually eased until she felt relatively normal, although more deeply relaxed than before. Then another wave of moving energy swept over her, followed by a wave of deep relaxation, this one reaching a bit further than the first. After a few minutes of rest, another wave followed. Every few minutes she felt a new wave of subtler, more delicate flow and release.

After about 30 minutes, she felt what she knew was the "last" wave. She dropped the handles of her copper biocircuit and stretched. She was so present, so rested, so alive.

A longtime meditator, he was at first skeptical of mind machines, but he decided to give one a try. He climbed into a reclining chair, donned goggles and headphones, and lay back.

As he adjusted to the sensation of the lightweight goggles resting on his nose, he took a deep breath. Soft music began and a splash of bright colors began dancing before his eyes in intricate geometric patterns. At first, he was amazed and fascinated by the complexity of the multi-colored light show, but as it continued, he noticed his body and mind relaxing as he slipped into a dreamlike state of rapture.

Soon, his body lay as if asleep, but his mind remained fully clear and awake, suspended in an inner peace whose stillness stood in stark contrast to the constant movement in the patterns of color that danced before him. The imagery was beautiful, and ever-changing. As he watched it changing, he noticed that he had begun to observe it all from a deeper place, a stable conscious "home" ~ it was such a familiar state, of course, he recognized it well from his years of sitting meditation practice...

How remarkable that this experience could be triggered by a machine, he thought ~ a "light and sound machine."

MICHAEL HUTCHISON & TERRY PATTEN

To an observer, she's just lying back on a recliner chair, but inwardly, she's swooning. She's not just "hearing" music, her whole body is tingling with pleasure from a sensual bath of sound and vibration. As the volume goes up, not only does the music fill her ears, but it seems to envelop her whole body, acting as a sonic massage, penetrating into every part of her being and bringing deep relaxation on all levels, physical, emotional and psychological.

With each exhalation, she relaxes even more profoundly, and the music seems to resonate more and more deeply, until she feels as though her body and mind are themselves vibrating every note. She is alternately enthralled by the delicious sensations of music dancing across her skin, and then swooning into a whole new plane of relaxation as she is transported by this all-consuming whole-body "trip". Goose bumps zing down her spine and shoulders, followed by a wave of profound "letting go."

Finally, after a half-hour of listening to nature sounds, rock & roll, new age and classical music, during the final crescendo of Pavarotti's trademark "Nessun Dorma," she begins crying uncontrollably. As she gets off the table, she says, "It's so wonderful, even sexual, and yet deeply moving. You know, I haven't been able to let myself go enough to feel this deeply in so long!"

Although her experience had more to do with her own inner emotions, and with the music she was hearing, it reached a profound depth because of the equipment she was using. It has many names ~ she was lying on a "sound table" or "musical bed" or was having a "vibro-tactile experience" on an "acoustic field generator."

Each of these experiences is unique, but in every one of them a person enters a profound state of pleasurable relaxation ~ a level of deep relaxation that is uncommon in our busy world ~ with the help of a new kind of technology.

TECHNOLOGY TO HELP YOU RECONNECT

Of course we need to relax. And in our computerized age, what can technology offer to make our relaxation fuller, more blissful, quicker, more luxurious, or more profound?

As we enter the new millennium our honeymoon with technology is over, replaced by a married-couple's passionate love-hate relationship. We spend endless hours in our cars, working and then playing on our computers, "nuking" our dinners in the microwave, talking on cordless and cellular phones, frequently feeling like victims of the very things that were supposed to make our lives easy. All-too-frequently our use of technology is part of a pattern that dissociates us from our bodies, our feelings, our souls ~ our consciousness.

But technology can also be a powerful servant for our reconnection to our bodies, our feelings, our souls, and our creative source. In fact, over the past decade a whole new category of technologies has emerged ~ mind or consciousness technologies ~ tools in which all the magic of computerization, microminiaturization, human engineering, biofeedback and neuroscience is put to the service of reconnecting us, relaxing us, and returning us to our own center.

What were a few isolated innovations ten years ago, has now become a fledgling industry. More and more people are using relaxation technologies every day. If professional trend-watchers like Faith Popcorn are right, these new consciousness technologies will inevitably be becoming a part of your life before the turn of the millennium.

A SPECTRUM OF TECHNOLOGIES

Relaxation technologies can function like "training wheels" enabling you to let go or enter relaxed meditative states more quickly or easily or deeply. With regular use, your body & mind "remember" the relaxation response and drop naturally into the state you've learned from the technology.

Some of these tools deprive you of stimuli. A floatation tank functions like a yogi's cave, isolating your attention from the myriad distractions that ordinarily stimulate you moment-to-moment. Others stimulate your body or brain with music, colors, electricity, sound, or light in a way that relaxes your body and/or mind. Biofeedback tools help you to notice subtle physiological signs of tension and relaxation, empowering you to intentionally control your level of relaxation at will. Others "do it for you" whether you notice or not; you simply take a "ride" to a more relaxed state.

MICHAEL HUTCHISON & TERRY PATTEN

Stillness Technologies

The first three relaxation technologies we describe are tools that do not stimulate you at all; instead they create an unusual state of unstimulation or stillness. In this category are floatation tanks and ganzfeld goggles. BioCircuits are described here too, because the experience of using them is most like these sensory-deprivation tools.

EXPLORING THE PRIVATE SEA ~ FLOATATION TANKS
After showering, you climb into a shallow tank of warm water laced with almost 1,000 pounds of epsom salts, creating a solution so dense your body floats on the surface like a cork, creating a sensation of near weightlessness. The water is maintained at body temperature, never feeling cool or warm. And neither does the air, which is separately warmed & ventilated. The lid shuts and you relax in darkness.

Ordinarily we experience a nearly constant stream of physical aches, pains, and incidental sensations. In the tank, these quickly subside and you find yourself alone, quiet, cut loose from the body's constant demands for attention. Your internal mental dialog stands out starkly, easily seen for what it is, just a subtler level of tension than your bodily stresses.

The "chattering monkey" soon quiets, permitting states of extraordinary lucidity, calmness and peace. Your internal experiences are all clear and vivid, just as the stars, which are rendered invisible by sunlight during the day, shine brightly on dark moonless nights.

Thus, the floatation tank has been acclaimed by one neuroscientist as "the most profound relaxation available on this planet" and by many consciousness explorers as the "supreme" tool for inner exploration. Can you imagine meditating with no body sensations to distract you, a reclining chair so comfortable that both you and the chair disappear, or massage so profound that the body sense literally dissolves?

Floatation Tanks start at just under $5,000 and deluxe models can cost over $13,000. However, it is possible (and plans are available) if you want, to build one yourself. In some cities, float centers "rent" time in a float tank for an average of approximately $40 per session.

GAZING INTO THE VOID ~ THE GANZFELD   You are gazing out into... light ~ a uniform, undifferentiated field of evenly illuminated but completely featureless visual space. This is a very unusual situation which we normally never experience.

Thoroughly researched, the ganzfeld generates "a 'turning off' of consciousness of the external world" according to Dr. Robert Ornstein, a research psychologist of Langley Porter Neuropsychiatric Institute. Our reticular activating system responds to the totally monotonous, unchanging, information-less ganzfeld first by boosting sensory acuity dramatically, then intensifying psychological awareness, and then into a profoundly intuitive "theta" brain state. (See chart on page 182-183).

As you gaze, your eyes naturally relax into a "soft focus." Although this is relaxing and soothing, nothing unusual happens, at least for the first twenty minutes or so. But then, the color gradually drains out of your vision, the light gradually seems to turn grey, starting at the periphery, and a misty space seems to open up. Soon it becomes hard to tell if your eyes are open or not. Your vision disappears altogether. You don't experience yourself looking at blackness, but rather "forget you have eyes."

During the next twenty minutes or so, you are lulled into a deeper and deeper state of relaxation characterized by strong theta waves. Parapsychological experiments show your intuitive powers are at their peak, and it is an ideal time for meditation, or for personal growth work or accelerated learning. After you slowly emerge from the ganzfeld, it seems as if the volume knob on your senses is turned way up ~ colors are vivid and saturated; sounds full, rich and intense; your skin is exquisitely sensitive.

As of this writing there is only one commercially-available ganzfeld device, retailing for $150.

MAKING THE ENERGY CONNECTION ~ BIOCIRCUITS   You lie on your back holding copper handles in each hand. They are connected by wires to copper pads placed underneath your sacrum, the base of your head, and the soles of your feet. You exhale, remembering to relax as completely as possible. At first, you experience nothing special, but after a few minutes, you notice your body begin twitching. Twitches and sensations of moving energy keep getting stronger and stronger.

Then there's a sudden, distinct wave of relaxation. Your rising agitation is gone, and you just feel a warm, deep wave of highly pleasurable relaxation.

This wave of relaxation gradually eases until you feel nothing unusual, although more relaxed than before you began. Then sensations of moving energy and agitation begin to build again. Once again, they peak and are swiftly followed by a wave of deep relaxation, this one going even farther than the first. After another few minutes, another wave builds, breaks, eases, and ends. For a full thirty minutes, you let these waves of tension and relaxation sweep over you, until somehow, you feel "finished." You let the copper handles drop from your hands, peacefully centered in an extraordinarily profound state of mental and physical relaxation.

Biocircuits are one of the smallest, simplest, easiest to use of all relaxation technologies. They can be bought inexpensively or built at home. Their relaxation effects have been demonstrated in double-blind experiments. But they're mysterious. Although we know that they're powerfully relaxing, we don't know why. Compared to other relaxation tools, the internal experience is most similar to the ganzfeld or to floating, in that there is no experience of external stimulation and the internal experience is still and centering.

Biocircuits are inexpensive, about $60, but extras and deluxe models can cost more.

Techno-Shamanism ~ the Light & Sound Machines

Push a button, and you suddenly see a kaleidoscopic pattern of complex, bright colors constantly dancing and shifting. These images can become dreamlike scenes of hypnagogic imagery, at times rich with emotion. Rhythmic sounds pulse in your ears, their volume set to be audible behind the music you chose for the occasion. And in the midst of this rush of sensation, you find yourself drifting into a state of profound relaxation, a stillness behind the dancing colors and sounds.

For millennia, dancing flames and the beat of drums have drawn human beings into trance, meditation, and ecstasy. One category of the new relaxation technologies (usually called "Light & Sound Machines") enables us to experience "fire-light" from goggles with flashing solid-state lights and "drumming" from synthesized digital sounds. You close your eyes and the goggles ignite a spectacular, internal kaleidoscopic light-show that draws you beyond mere visual experience into any of several sometimes-trancelike states of profound relaxation, creativity, or alertness.

Your own internal experience shifts distinctly when the light flashes change frequencies. New colors appear, different intricate moving geometric patterns replace those you saw previously, and your own internal state of consciousness begins to alter as well. Light and Sound machines enable you to tune in your shamanic journey created by precisely-controlling the rhythms and frequencies of the electronic "drumming and fire-light."

These machines first appeared about twenty years ago, and in the past decade have become affordably-priced ($100-$400) consumer products. Current versions offer a wide range of features. Most let you choose from a range of inbuilt "programs" (sequences of changing frequency settings) each of

which can be directed towards a particular purpose (relaxation, sleep, creativity, visualization, learning, etc.) Some let
you create and store, or even edit your own programs. Some
let you control the speed of the flashes manually, so you can
play around and explore the effects of different frequencies.
Some have brighter lights, a wider range of internal sounds.
Almost all let you plug in music from your CD or cassette
player.

Light & Sound machines have become one of the most popular consciousness technologies, partly because they are so
entertaining, and partly because they are so easy to use. You
just put on the goggles and headphones and push a few but-
tons. Your experience begins. It's as close as our age has come
to "electronic relaxation on demand."

Of all categories of relaxation technologies, Light & Sound
machines offer the greatest range of choices. Many different
models are currently available, at prices ranging from $100 to
$600. All offer a selection of inbuilt "programs." Starting at
$150, some let you manually control the frequency of the light
flashes. Starting at just under $300, some models let you cre-
ate your own programs and store them for future use. Certain
machines (but none with manual operation or programmabil-
ity) accept audiotapes with coded programs, some coordinat-
ing the light flashes with recordings of music, nature sounds
and voice. Others can be controlled by your computer, allowing
tremendously sophisticated control of a multitude of parame-
ters. Some different kinds of goggles or headphones. Some
have dedicated tapes (for accelerated learning or weight control, for instance).

Before purchasing a Light & Sound machine, consider
whether you just want it for relaxation and recreation or
whether you want to explore all its possibilities. This will help
you decide how wide a selection of programs you need,
whether you care if your machine allows manual operation or
user-programmability, whether you care how fully you will be
able to control the unit, and how important price is to you.

Tuning In to Your Body ~ Biofeedback

Biofeedback has been called the "first western yoga" because
it teaches you to pay attention to your body on a subtle level,

and even to control the body's subtle functions, much as yogis do via meditation, breath control, hatha yoga, and disciplines of attention.

Of all the means of relaxation described in this book, none is more "pure" than biofeedback. Biofeedback makes you aware of your body at levels far beyond your usual awareness and control, and it creates a simple way for you to learn how to relax your capillaries, chronic muscle tension, or brainwaves. In biofeedback, you literally learn a new skill; you learn how to relax tension you usually couldn't perceive, something you later practice very profitably in the midst of stressful life circumstances.

You're sitting quietly, relaxing, with sensors attached to your head, watching a TV screen with a Pac Man game display. As your brainwave activity shows increases in relaxed "theta" activity, Mr. Pac Man gobbles more and more rapidly, moving through the maze, and "winning" the game. As your theta brainwaves decrease, he slows down, and you start "losing." You were told to try to win at Pac Man but cautioned that the best way to do this is to "allow" the game to win itself, not to "make it" happen.

So you sit there, "relaxing." At first it's easy. Mr. Pac Man chomps faster and faster, and you quickly reach the next level. Then your success seems to stop. On level two, Mr. Pac Man seems listless, and stays that way. You try to get him moving by relaxing more. But he freezes up and goes retro. What's wrong? You're stumped; why isn't it working? The clock ticks by as you watch your score become ever more dismal.

You take a deep breath and decide not to let it bother you. Soon, your Pac Man figure comes to life, and you get a feel for how to sustain him.

This time you notice what you were thinking, what you were doing with your attention, and how you were feeling while Mr. Pac Man was chomping ever faster. You tune in to a certain inner flow that was just moving, and a subtle tension that ordinarily seems to block it. So you let that tension continue to relax and shift in the same way, letting it go even further. Sure enough: Pac Man wins in record time. You've popped into level three. You "allow" Pac Man to do what he does best, watching with a dreamy, bemused smile on your face. You're beginning to feel really relaxed.

One of the central assumptions of western physiology has been that there is a fundamental distinction between parts of the human body that we can consciously control ~ the so-called "voluntary" components ~ and those parts over which we have no conscious control ~ the "involuntary" components. These involuntary components traditionally included such things as the expansion and contraction of our blood vessels, our blood pressure, heart rate, the secretion of hormones, the activity of our immune system, and even our brain wave patterns.

THE VOLUNTARY VS. THE INVOLUNTARY & THE DISCOVERY OF THE BODY MIND   Then a lightning bolt hit. With the development of sensitive instruments that could measure minute changes in the body, scientists found that if they monitored the activity of one of the so-called involuntary processes of a human subject and fed it back to that subject with some sort of visual or auditory signal, the subject could learn to bring that process under voluntary control. They called this process biofeedback.

In a burst of studies that caused a sensation in the scientific world, biofeedback researchers proved that subjects could take voluntary control of virtually any physiological process ~ even the firing rhythm of individual nerve cells. Elder and Alyce Green of the Menninger Foundation wrote with excitement, "It may be possible to bring under some degree of voluntary control any physiological process that can continuously be monitored, amplified, and displayed."

This was a momentous discovery ~ it meant that the long-held belief of a clear separation between voluntary and involuntary components of the human system was not accurate. It meant such process as the secretion of hormones and the operation of the immune system could theoretically be intentionally controlled. It also meant that the whole foundation of mind-body dualism upon which all of western thought had been based ~ that there was a clear and necessary separation between the mind and the body ~ had to go out the window. For clearly there was some link, still mysterious, between mind and body.

It was the beginning of a great paradigm shift that was to lead to the development of such fields as psychoneuroimmunology and psychobiology, and to the emergence of a new vision of the mind and body as a single, indivisible unit, a field of intelligence, a bodymind.

PRACTICAL TOOLS FOR PROFOUND RELAXATION Aside from the theoretical implications, it quickly became clear that the breakthroughs in biofeedback had enormous practical applications. Using temperature biofeedback, migraine sufferers could learn to make their hands warmer, thus increasing peripheral blood flow, and alleviating the migraine. People with heart malfunctions learned to control their heart rates. Biofeedback training was effective in helping people lower their blood pressure, control gastrointestinal problems such as ulcers, excess stomach acidity and irritable bowel syndrome, and alleviate problems associated with muscle tension, such as teeth grinding, jaw and joint problems, tension headache, cerebral palsy, paralysis resulting from brain damage and much more.

More generally, researchers found that many different types of biofeedback instruments, including those that measured skin temperature (abbreviated TEMP), muscle tension (called electromyographs, or EMGs), and the electrical conductivity of the skin (GSR or EDR meters), were powerful tools for teaching people to become deeply relaxed. In many cases subjects could learn to quickly put themselves into states of profound relaxation with only a few biofeedback training sessions. Using biofeedback relaxation training, researchers were able to produce a wide variety of positive psychological as well as physiological effects, including alleviation of phobias and anxiety and increases in IQ.

The power unleashed by biofeedback is not in the equipment, but in opening new levels of physical awareness. When you practice biofeedback, you learn important new relaxation skills because you develop much greater sensitivity to your own body. As you follow the biofeedback signal and "tune in" to what you must do to change that signal, you are becoming much more sensitive to your nervous system, to your musculature or to your underlying level of arousal, and you are learning to exert voluntary control over "involuntary" psycho-physiological stress.

PROFESSIONAL BIOFEEDBACK & DO-IT-YOURSELF Although biofeedback is relatively new, there are now skilled biofeedback practitioners in private practice all over the world. Usually their patients are referred by doctors, or they may work in association with a doctor or hospital. If you think biofeedback is for you, ask your doctor to refer you to a biofeedback practitioner in your own community.

Biofeedback practitioners guide patients through biofeedback sessions that help them learn to reduce anxiety, stress, or the experience of chronic pain. They also teach people with insomnia how to fall asleep. Some new biofeedback protocols help people break patterns of addiction to cigarettes, drugs and alcohol. Additionally, biofeedback is being used increasingly to cure phobias and also to help people with learning disabilities. Even when the goal is very sophisticated, most professional biofeedback trainings begin by helping clients simply learn how to relax more deeply.

Probably the most "sexy" and rapidly-advancing area of biofeedback is brainwave biofeedback. New protocols may revolutionize problems with addiction, depression and learning disabilities. There is evidence that the learning and self-regulation process of EEG training, whatever the target frequency, beta, alpha, theta, left-right hemisphere synchrony, or even site-specific activation training, "organizes" brainwave activity that seems to boost the brain into optional functioning and increases intelligence, or IQ.

If you'd like to tune in to your body or brain on deeper level and learn how to relax more profoundly, there are some affordable biofeedback tools you can use at home (priced below $100). Most of these show you your tension or relaxation via an audible tone. Usually, like in the example at the beginning of this section, you relax by "allowing" the pitch of that tone to get deeper. Sometimes the feedback is visual, in the form of a meter needle reading, a changing digital numeric display, or a changing video pattern. Simple TEMP, GSR or EMG biofeedback tools for personal use can be purchased for $60 to $100. More sophisticated tools exist, and even the simplest EEG biofeedback devices cost $1,000 to $4,000.

PASSIVE BIOFEEDBACK   The field of biofeedback has seen exciting advances in recent years. There are now many kinds of brainwave (EEG) biofeedback including alpha and theta training, which both teach relaxation, but also various types of beta training which activate specific parts of the brain and have shown tremendous promise as treatments for hyperactivity and attention-deficit disorder (ADD). One new modality that combines EEG feedback with Light & Sound stimulation to produce a feedback/feedforward loop is called "EEG Disentrainment Feedback" (or EDF). It flashes lights in a pair of goggles at the frequency of the dominant brainwave pattern measured via EEG. However, unlike traditional EEG biofeedback, the subject makes no attempt to modify his or her brainwaves. The EEF process itself seems to produce dramatic positive therapeutic changes.

Similarly, breath feedback works passively. You lie back, relax, and breathe normally, and you "hear" and "see" each breath cycle via lights and sounds. The repeated experience of your natural breathing rhythm becomes hypnotic, lulling you into a deeply relaxed "twilight" state between waking and sleeping which some researchers have correlated with measurements of "theta" dominant brainwave states. In fact, some researchers believe that the simple, passive process of breath feedback is the fastest and most reliable way yet found to enter into theta-dominant "twilight" brainwave states.

Biofeedback practitioners charge anywhere from $40 to $150 per session (usually $60-$75 for one hour).

The Subtle, Sublime Pleasures of Motion

It's a bit like a baby might feel when being rocked, comforting, and subtly playful somehow, with a sense as though you are floating in space. You find yourself letting go, just enjoying the ride, feeling almost as though you are sweetly being carried to an inner destination.

You experience a delicious deja-vu, a sudden demonstration that motion itself can bequeath a potent sense of well-being. And you realize that you are grinning like an idiot, swooning in this motion, no stronger, no more exaggerated than that of a raft gently bobbing on the surface of a lake.

What's causing this experience? You are simply reclining on a "motion chair." When it is switched on, you and the chair begin gently moving in a continuous tilting orbit of about six inches in diameter.

Another technique for relaxing the brain is physical movement, stimulation of our natural balance-sensing mechanism, the vestibular system of our inner ear canals. Research with laboratory animals kept motionless, and humans who have been immobilized, has provided dramatic evidence of the crucial importance of movement to human development and mental-physical well-being. From the time of our conception, movement is an essential nutrient: without it, the brain does not develop fully. As babies we are rocked, as kids we run, jump, roll down hills and spin until we're dizzy, as adults we play sports, drive fast around turns, dance and, when tired, sit in rocking chairs. This movement is not only pleasurable, but simultaneously relaxes and stimulates our body and nervous system. Like light and sound, motion is a nutrient for the brain and body, and if we consistently fall short of meeting our minimum daily requirement, we become susceptible to stress and chronic health problems.

One major effect of movement is that it stimulates the fluids of the inner ear, known as the vestibular system. This stimulation sends a flood of electrical impulses into our cerebellum and from there into the rest of the brain, including the pleasure and learning centers of the limbic system.

Certain kinds of movement are disturbing; others are soothing. All provide the brain with stimulation. Certain patterns are especially deeply relaxing, even making the user feel "stoned." These have led to the development of a variety of "motion systems" that keep the user moving constantly, providing vestibular stimulation ~ and brain exercise ~ in a concentrated form.

A number of "motion systems" are now commercially available, including reclining chairs that slowly rise, tilt, dip, and retilt (at about 2 to 3 rpm), beds that gently tilt, revolve, and rock, and chairs that gently spin.

The most powerfully relaxing of these systems creates a very small and gentle movement ~ with a gently huge effect. One writer has called the effect "tidal weightlessness." EEGs

The brain is powered by electricity. Each of its billions of individual cells "fires" or electrically discharges at a specific frequency. The electrical activity of the brain can be monitored by placing sensors or electrodes against the scalp, which register the minute electrical signals happening inside the brain, much the way a seismograph can detect tremors taking place inside the earth. The device that registers these signals is called an electroencephalograph, or EEG. What the EEG measures are not the firings of individual brain cells, but the cooperative or collective electrical patterns of networks or communities of millions of cells firing together, fluctuations of energy sweeping across the networks of the brain. These collective energy pulsations are called brain waves.

Since the first EEG was devised in the 1920s, scientists have found that the brain has a tendency to produce brain waves of four distinct varieties, which they have called beta, alpha, theta and delta.

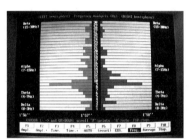

BETA

14 to 100 cycles per second (Hz). In our normal waking state, eyes open, focusing on the world outside ourselves or working on concrete, specific problems, beta waves (particularly 14-40 Hz) are dominant and powerful. Beta waves are an important sign of the mature human brain (as contrasted with theta-dominant patterns seen in children.) Beta-dominant brainwave states are associated with alertness, arousal, concentration, cognition and, when excessive, anxiety.

ALPHA

8 to 13 Hz. As we close our eyes and become more relaxed, passive, or unfocused, brainwave activity slows and we produce bursts of alpha waves. If we become quite relaxed and mentally unfocused, alpha waves

Brain States

become dominant throughout the brain, producing a calm and pleasant sensation called "the alpha state." The alpha state seems to be the brain's "neutral" or idling state, and people who are healthy and not under stress tend to produce a lot of alpha activity. Lack of significant alpha activity can be a sign of anxiety, stress, brain damage or illness.

THETA

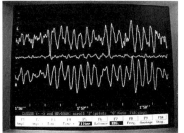

4 to 8 Hz. As calmness and relaxation deepen into drowsiness, the brain shifts to slower, more powerfully rhythmic theta waves. Theta dominant brainwave states have been called "twilight states" between waking and sleep. They're often accompanied by unexpected, dreamlike mental images. Theta offers access to unconscious material, reveries, free association, sudden insight and creative ideas. It's a mysterious, elusive state, and for a long time experimenters had a difficult time studying it because it is hard to maintain over time ~ most people tend to fall straight into the delta dominant brainwave patterns of sleep as soon as they begin generating large amounts of theta.

DELTA

As we fall asleep, our dominant brain waves become delta, which are even slower than theta. When delta waves become dominant most people are either asleep or otherwise unconscious. However, there is growing evidence that individuals may maintain consciousness while in a delta dominant state. This seems to be associated with extremely deep meditation or other "non physical" states. It is while we're in delta-dominant brainwave states that our brains release large quantities of human growth hormone (HGH).

of users show that these units can produce rapid, dramatic, and long-lasting changes. Most subjects seem to show increases in slow brainwave activity, enhanced neural efficiency quotients (correlated with higher IQ) and a higher degree of brainwave coherence (phase synchrony of brain activity across both hemispheres).

Motion-chairs and beds are expensive ~ $4000 to $13,000. Vibro-tactile tables and chairs are also fairly costly ~ they start at $2,000 and some of the most deluxe units cost well over $10,000 ~ although there is one simple new unit (it looks like a massage table without legs) that costs only $700.

Sound Tables & Musical Chairs ~ The Ultimate Relaxation Machines?

You recline, relax, and let go. Music begins, but not just for your ears. The surface upon which you're lying begins tingling your whole body in a sensory bath of sound and vibration, playing upon your skin with the constantly changing vibrations of the music. And the music itself keeps changing, cycling through a wide array of styles. Sometimes the melodies, textures and rhythms feel soothing, sometimes powerful and intense, and sometimes exquisite and sublime. Through it all, you only relax more and more deeply, letting go into a musical experience that seems to take over your whole being. You are lying on a bed, table, or chair equipped with speakers or transducers and transformed into a "Whole Body Acoustic Field Generator" also known as a "Sound Table," "Musical Bed" (or "Musical Chair"), or "Vibro-Tactile Stimulator."

These devices have "blown the minds" of many users; in their wake we find a striking concentration of enthusiastic, emphatic praise, strong claims, and testimonials laced with superlatives. Designers of several sound tables have deliberately attempted to create an "ultimate consciousness machine" or something close.

One researcher, Dr. Jeffrey Thompson, has pointed out that a huge section of the brainstem and nervous system is devoted to sensing and processing vibration. The spinal cord is composed of nerve bundles carrying different kinds of sensation such as heat and cold, pain, pressure, vibration, etc. Two entire columns sense vibration and take up almost the whole posterior half of the spinal cord. Large portions of the deep, primitive portions of the brain near the brainstem are devoted to vibration-processing. "So when you are lying on a sound table, powerful emotional information, in the form of musical vibrations, gets processed right in the part of the brain where our most deep-seated emotional programs reside. This is one reason sound tables produce such powerful effects."

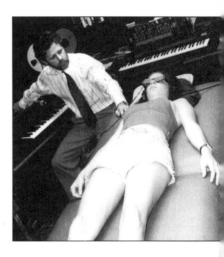

Another sound table enthusiast, Byron Eakin, emphasizes the sensuous novelty of the experience: "Feeling music in the body is a unique experience; we're just not used to it. This has a profound effect. It really gets your attention. And if you 'let go' into the experience, all kinds of things can happen… I've heard people describe emotional catharsis, mystical experiences, out-of-body travel, amazing things."

Another innovator, Don Estes, emphasizes the fact that these units stimulate the brain, via the skin and the ears, with a large volume of completely congruent information. Normally, in order to focus on a single stimulus, your reticular activating system has to screen out countless "background" sensations. Estes says, "When the music 'drowns out' the background distractions, the attention and mental energy that would otherwise be used up by the task of sorting inputs, is freed up. This in itself is highly unusual, and it means you have much more consciousness available than you would ordinarily."

"And what is presented to consciousness? Music. And great music is profound. Music is the greatest form of communication man has ever created. Music can be emotionally powerful, aesthetically powerful, mentally pleasurable, physically healing, deeply relaxing. And consciousness is uniquely freed up. No wonder the result is so profound."

Dr. Patrick Flanagan points out, "Each cavity in the body is a Helholtz resonator; it has a specific frequency to which it resonates like a tuning fork. Thus, if the body is resonated by music, certain parts of the body will resonate particularly strongly to each frequency."

Over the last few decades, far-seeing researchers have studied the effects of coherent sound on human consciousness. Since the time of the Vedas of ancient India, explorers of consciousness have agreed that sound can influence how we think, feel, cognize, behave, and exist. In the last twenty years, a vocabulary of psycho-acoustic techniques has taken shape. Among these new technologies are the following:

BINAURAL BEATS   are continuous tones of slightly different frequency, or pitch, which can be heard on the left and right channels of a recording. If the left channel tone is "A-440" (440 cycles per second) and the right channel tone is 448 cycles per second, the difference between the two, 8 cycles per second, can be heard as a gentle, pulsing, "wah-wah" sound.

PULSED TONES   are rhythmic, pulsing sounds which are mixed into a recording to stimulate the listener at a particular frequency. Pulsed tones are usually white noise or a synthesizer tone, but they can also emulate the natural sounds such as cricket chirps or the rhythmic splattering of raindrops.

FREQUENCY EFFECTS   are created using binaural beats or pulsed sounds. These are usually patterned based on brainwave frequencies, so that the listener's brainwaves may easily fall into sync with the sound frequency patterns. These can fall into beta wave frequencies (13 cycles per second and above), alpha frequencies (8-12 cycles per second), theta frequencies (4-8 cycles per second) or delta frequencies (.5 to 4 cycles per second).

WINDOW FREQUENCIES   also relate to binaural beat or pulsed-tone technology. Certain specific brainwave frequencies (or combinations of frequencies) are associated with highly specific states of consciousness. These same frequencies can be created using binaural beats or pulsed sounds, and this, in turn, may make it easier for listeners to enter into the same specific states of consciousness.

TOMATIS ENHANCEMENT   techniques involve emphasizing certain frequencies as per the teachings of Dr. Alfred Tomatis, the innovative French ear surgeon. Tomatis teaches that certain types of sounds "charge the brain" and energize the whole organism. His system of understanding is rich and complex, and it has been particularly applied to train the voice, with resulting improvements in overall health, learning abilities, and the sense of hearing. Tomatis particularly praises Gregorian Chants and the music of Mozart, and he emphasizes the value of sounds rich in overtones and sounds which are carried to our brains through bone conduction (chiefly frequencies above 2000 Hz). Tomatis developed a device he calls the "electronic ear" which is used to reeducate the ear by amplifying certain frequencies. Making use of some of Tomatis' insights, music or other sounds can be specially treated to create beneficial effects in the listener.

Acoustics

PRIMORDIAL SOUNDS are sounds to which humans have been exposed throughout our long history as a species. Some innovative sound healers believe that certain primordial sounds may be deeply encoded into our psychology and physiology and that hearing them evokes powerful responses. They are viewed as the sonic equivalents of collectively-recognized symbols or archetypes such as those explored by Jungian psychologists. Most of these sounds are experienced as familiar and comforting, perhaps because they are familiar not just to each individual, but to our entire evolutionary heritage. Examples of primordial sounds are the human heartbeat, crickets, a crackling fire, rain and ocean surf.

3D SOUNDS are sounds of any kind that have been captured and recorded using special 3-D microphones. Especially effective when heard through headphones, these recordings enable the listener to experience sounds in precise locations in three-dimensional acoustic space. Environmental sounds recorded with the 3D technique possess greatly enhanced realism. Any sound can be placed and moved in and around the head and body so that specific sounds are experienced in specific subjective "places" which may enhance or alter your experience of them.

Sounds may be placed in space according to any of several rationales. For example, Neuro-Linguistic Programming (NLP) theory identifies the habitual spatial placement of certain types of thought or feeling processes. The esoteric anatomy of India identifies the seven "chakras" arranged from the base of the spine to the crown of the head, each corresponding to a level of gross or subtle human activity, experience, and consciousness. Using either of these systems, or perhaps others, sounds may be placed so that the way their effects are experienced is enhanced by their perceived location in space.

Of course, all of the above psycho-acoustic techniques are most often combined with music, which is a vast, rich, wonderful language in itself. Since music can move us on emotional, sensual, psychological and spiritual levels, it can influence our physiology by making it easy for us to relax or by arousing us, and it influences our consciousness in many ways. Highly predictable or unpredictable music affects us very differently. Music can demand that we pay close attention to it, or it can invite us to let it recede into the background of our attention and affect us apart from our conscious participation. Thus, music should not be imagined to be a "minor" ingredient in psycho-acoustic recordings. Also, psycho-acoustic recordings sometimes use music in combination with environmental sounds, binaural beats, and other sound enhancement techniques. Thus there can also be synergy among these techniques, which can create another order of effects.

"The modality is inherently powerful, in part because the human skin is such a powerful sense organ. Our skin is not just a covering; it is an enormously sensitive organ with hundreds of thousands of receptors for temperature and vibrotactile input. Every organ of perception develops ontologically and phylogenetically out of skin. In the embryo skin folds and then form our eyes and our ears. Our skin may contain the latent capacity to perceive light and sound. I think by stimulating the skin with energy in the right way, you can potentially repolarize the brain and charge it with energy."

Regardless of what the experts say, it is obvious that when you deeply relax and your whole body is bathed in musical vibration, you are immersed and carried by music in a way that is extraordinarily sensuous, ecstatic and relaxing.

BRINGING RELAXATION BACK HOME

You feel a gentle vibration, signaling you to remember. You take a deep breath; you check your posture; you stretch your spine from side to side, and you let go of the tension you notice in your face and hands. Mentally, you give thanks for the little tool that has been reminding you all day to "just do it" ~ relax, that is, regardless of what particular stressful circumstance you're in when it signals you. It has made you so much more aware of your daily cycles of uptightness, and it has felt so healthy to confront those moments directly, by relaxing in the midst of them.

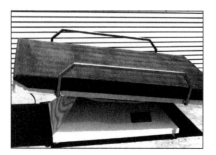

We feel it's important to mention one tool that was created specifically for "bridging the gap" between those moments of deep relaxation and the stress patterns of daily living. It is a timer with a vibrator attached, a pager-sized unit that you place in your pocket or clip to your belt. A simple device, useful for remembering anything you want to be reminded of repeatedly throughout the day ~ to correct your posture, take a deep breath, have a glass of water, say your mantra, remember your spiritual inspiration, or relax (and most of these things relate in one way or another to relaxation).

We tend to get swept up in our daily activities and forget to do the things we "know" we really want to do. This simple piece of technology breaks through this pattern of forgetting, enabling us to integrate relaxation into the rest of our daily life.

USING, ENJOYING, & EXPLORING NEW RELAXATION TECHNOLOGIES

A rich array of new technologies can make it easier or quicker to relax; they can help you reach more pleasurable or more profound states of relaxation; or they can help you integrate relaxation into the rest of your day.

Many are quite affordable (most can be obtained for less than $100). A few, however, are very expensive (floatation tanks, motion machines, and most vibro-tactile tables and chairs cost $2,000 or more). Most of these tools are easy to use, but some (many forms of EEG biofeedback, for example) require the help of a technically sophisticated operator. At the end of this chapter you'll find listings for a wide range of resources.

The first thing to remember about these tools is that they are all serving a relaxation process that is natural to you and that is inherent in every human bodymind. They can represent powerful help, potent ingredients in the human alchemy of relaxation and pleasure ~ but they should be approached with a healthy attitude. And what is that? Approach them with openness, curiosity, and the intention to be delighted. These technologies cannot give you anything that is not natural to you; when they connect, they just serve your natural capacity for pleasure, relaxation, reconnection to your body, your feelings, your source and your soul.

Tools for Relaxation

A Resource Guide

MEDITATION

BOOKS

The Relaxation Response
Herbert Benson, M.D.
Morrow And Company, 1975.
A landmark work that popularized meditation for a Western audience.

Beyond the Relaxation Response
Herbert Benson, M.D.
Avon, 1975.
Stress reduction techniques to cure health problems without drugs.

The Quiet Mind: Techniques for Transforming Stress
John Harvey, Ph.D.
Himalayan Publishers, 1988.
Draws on perspectives of contemporary psychology and wisdom to examine the role of the mind in the stress problem.

Minding The Body, Mending the Mind
Joan Borysenko, Ph.D.
Bantam, 1987.
A mind/body approach to stress management and meditation.

Full Catastrophe Living
Jon Kabat-Zinn, Ph.D.
Delta, 1990.
Using the wisdom of your body and mind to face stress, pain, and illness.

Mind as a Healer, Mind as a Slayer
Kenneth Pelletier
Delta, 1977.
An in-depth approach to healing through meditation.

How to Meditate
Lawrence LeShan
Bantam, 1974.
Proven programs and exercises that allow you to bring meditation into your life despite distractions or demands on your time.

Increasing Executive Productivity
P. Neurenberger
Prentice Hall, 1992.
A source book on meditation and personal effectiveness.

Journey of Awakening: A Meditator's Guidebook
Ram Dass
Bantam, 1978.
A good beginner's guide to meditation and the literature about it.

Yoga Psychology: A Practical Guide to Meditation
S. Ajaya
Himalayan, 1976.
An excellent introduction to the practice, philosophy and psychology of meditation.

Zen Mind, Beginners Mind
S. Suzuki
Weatherhill, 1977.
A classic work valuable throughout your practice of meditation.

Meditation and Its Practice
Swami Rama
Himalayan Publishers, 1992.
A practical, comprehensive guide to meditation that will benefit beginners as well as those who want to deepen their meditative experience.

The Miracle of Mindfulness: A Manual on Meditation
T. N. Hanh
Beacon Press, 1976.
A beautiful and enduring classic on meditation.

The Textbook of Yoga Psychology
Translated By R. Mishra
Julian Press, 1987.
A basic yoga text containing very clear information on meditation
and associated practices along with psychological and spiritual
implications.

RECORDINGS

Mindfulness Meditation Practice
Jon Kabat-Zinn, Ph.D.
P.O. Box 547
Lexington, MA   02173
Six tapes in a series containing specific guided meditations with
techniques such as silence with bells to mark the passage of time,
guided body scan and guided yoga.

Meditation: An Invitation to Inner Growth
Swami Chetanananda
Rudra Press
Learn to meditate with this audio program by a highly respected
american master of Trika yoga.

SOURCES FOR PRODUCT

The Sounds True Catalog
735 Walnut Street Dept SC94
Boulder, CO   80302
800 333-9185
CDs, cassettes, videotapes and spoken word tapes on creativity,
self-discovery, psychology, relationships, meditation and more.

ORGANIZATIONS

Stress Reduction Clinic
Jon Kabat-Zinn, Ph.D.
P.O. Box 547
University Of Mass Medical Center
Lexington, MA   02173
508-856-2656
The oldest and largest hospital-based stress reduction clinic in the
country. An outpatient behavioral medicine clinic in the form of an
eight-week long course that you can take as a complement to whatever medical treatments you may be receiving. People are referred
to clinic with conditions such as: chronic pain, high blood pressure,
cancer, AIDS, and fatigue.

YOGA

Lilias, Yoga and Your Life
Lilias Folan
Rudra Press
Hundreds of Hatha yoga exercises and a week-by-week progressive schedule with 150 instructive photographs.

Dynamic Stillness Part One: The Practice of Trika Yoga
Swami Chetanananda
Rudra Press
A candid and reliable guide to modern spiritual work to release tensions, explore energy centers, and connect to the flow of creative energy within.

Dynamic Stillness Part Two: The Fulfillment of Trika Yoga
Swami Chetanananda
Rudra Press
A deeper look into the experience of our inner self including living from the highest awareness possible.

Stretch and Relax: A Day By Day Workout and Relaxation Program
M. Tobias and M. Stewart
The Body Press, 1985.
A step-by-step program to working out and relaxing.

Hatha Yoga or the Yogi Philosophy of Physical Well-Being
Yogi Ramacharaka
Yogi Publication Society, 1930.
A foundation upon which the student may build a sound, strong, and healthy body through Hatha yoga.

RECORDINGS

Rest, Relax and Sleep
Lilias Folan
Rudra Press
A three tape audio set and booklet to revitalize during your day with yoga stretches, conscious breathing, mindfulness, and visualization.

Yoga with Lilias: For Beginning Students
Lilias Folan
Rudra Press
60-minute audio tape with illustrated guide.

REST
RELAX
AND
SLEEP

Lilias
Folan

PBS-TV's
Relaxation Expert
Presents a New
Six-Week Program
For a Good
Night's Sleep

Yoga with Lilias: For Experienced Students
Lilias Folan
Rudra Press
Two audio tapes include a two-hour yoga program with illustrated guide.

VIDEOS

Yoga for Round Bodies Vol. 1, Vol. 2
Demarco And Haddon
Rudra Press
Two 90-minute videos of gentle yoga instruction.

Tri-Yoga, Level 1
Kali Ray
Rudra Press
A flowing yoga practice designed to build flexibility, strength, endurance, tone muscles, increase mental alertness and energy levels.

Yogarobics
Larry Lane
Rudra Press
A low-impact aerobic routine based on dance-type movements with some yoga postures and attention to inner awareness.

Alive with Yoga Vol.1, Vol. 2
Lilias Folan
Rudra Press
Two 60-minute video tapes starting with beginning yoga stretches and working up to more challenging flexibility on volume 2.

Forever Flexible
Lilias Folan
Rudra Press
Ageless, all level exercises especially for those with limitations in joints or back.

Lilias! Energize with Yoga
Lilias Folan
Goldhil Video, 1993.
Two dynamic 30-minute yoga workouts for all levels.

Forward Bends
Manouso Manos
Rudra Press
Detailed voice instructtion and excellent visual presentation of a variety of seated poses for beginners and advanced students.

Join PBS–TV yoga expert Lilias Folan for an invigorating daily yoga practice for all levels and tap your greatest resource – your own energy!

The Inversions
Manouso Manos
Rudra Press
A thorough presentation of the inverted yoga postures.

The Standing Poses
Manouso Manos
Rudra Press
14 standing poses taught with clarity, precision, and grace.

Yoga for Beginners
Patricia Walden
Rudra Press
75-minute video that leads you through beginning hatha yoga in a slow and easy-to-follow way.

Yoga Practice for Flexibility
Patricia Walden
Rudra Press
One of three tapes in a series for your complete home practice based on movement, conditioning, and relaxation.

Yoga Practice for Relaxation
Patricia Walden And Rodney Yee
Rudra Press
The third tape in a series allowing you to expand the relaxation portion of your yoga practice.

Yoga Practice for Strength
Rodney Yee
Rudra Press
One of three tapes in a series. Builds strength while energizing your body and stimulating your mind.

Children's Yoga with Animals
Thia Luby
Myriad Images
P.O. Box 6008
Santa Fe, NM   87502
505 438-0793
60-minute yoga video featuring animals followed by children copying the animal movements with yoga stretches.

Aerobic Yoga: The Flow Series
White And Rich
Rudra Press
Aimed at the intermediate to advanced, a complete workout designed to build strength, muscle tone and stamina.

Yoga International
717 253-6241
Magazine that offers the best features on yoga, mediatation, health, and spirituality. First issue free.

Yoga Journal
2054 University Ave
Berkeley, CA   94704
510 841-9200
Dedicated to communicating the qualities of being that yoga exemplifies: peace, integrity, clarity, and compassion. Focuses on body/mind approaches to personal and spiritual development.

SOURCES FOR PRODUCT

Rudra Press
P.O. Box 13390
Portland, OR   97213-0390
800 876-7798 or 800-394-6286
Publishes health, meditation, and yoga books and videos. Free catalog available.

FOOD FOR RELAXATION

BOOKS

Food and Healing
Annemarie Colbin
Ballantine, 1986.
An overview of the various ways in which food affects health, based on Eastern and Western models of thought, with a section on foods that heal headaches, colds, stomach aches and other conditions.

The Book of Whole Meals
Annemarie Colbin
Ballantine, 1983.
A mostly vegetarian cookbook, using whole grains, beans, vegetables, and fruits, that lays out dinner, breakfast, and lunch made with the leftovers from dinner; six days for each season, a total of twenty-four of each of the meals.

The Natural Gourmet
Annemarie Colbin
Ballantine, 1989.
A mostly vegetarian cookbook, with chapters on appetizers, soups, grain dishes, bean dishes, vegetables, salads, fish, and sugar-free desserts, all classified according to the Chinese theory of the Five Phases.

Tofu Tollbooth
A Directory Of Great Natural And Organic Food Stores
Dar Williams
Ardwork Press
A directory of over 300 cooperative natural food stores around the country.

Food - Your Miracle Medicine
Jean Carper
Harpercollins, 1993.
Details the medicinal powers of food that can be used every day to prevent and alleviate such common maladies as headaches, hay fever and arthritic pain, as well as to ward off heart disease and cancer.

The Food Pharmacy
Jean Carper
Bantam,1988.
A fascinating guide to understanding what folklore has proclaimed for centuries and science is now confirming: that food is powerful medicine.

Managing Your Mind and Mood Through Food
Judith Wurtman, Ph.D. With Margaret Danbrot
Rawson Associates, 1986.
Explains the neurotransmitter theory in layman's language, shows how to eat to control mood swings, stress and jet lag, the judicious use of caffeine and carbohydrate snacks, and offers various recipes and menus to illustrate the points made.

The Healing Herbs: The Ultimate Guide to the Curative Powers of Nature's Medicines
Michael Castleman
Rodale Press, 1991.
Extensive listing of 100 healing herbs, with chapters on the historical use of herbs, safety, storing and preparing herbal products, and how to obtain them, including gathering, growing, and purchasing herbs.

Macrobiotic Home Remedies
Michio Kushi
Japan Publications, 1985.
Includes a theoretical approach based on the yin/yang model and the concept of Ki (Chi), and an extensive list of home remedies such as special foods, teas, plasters, compresses, juices, and baths for all manner of conditions, including coughs, hemorrhoids, fevers, diarrhea, bleeding, and diabetes.

*The Vegetarian Journal's Guide to Natural Foods Restaurants
    in the U.S. and Canada*
Vegetarian Resource Group, Avery, 1993.
410 366-VEGE
A listing of over 1,500 natural foods restaurants, vegetarian inns,
spas, camps, and vacation spots. Also lists addresses of active local
vegetarian groups.

ORGANIZATIONS

The Natural Gourmet Institute for Food and Health
48 West 21 Street 2nd Floor
New York, NY   10010
212 645-5170
Offers a wide range of training classes, lectures, workshops, tapes,
books, and products focused on natural foods cooking, health and
entrepreneurial pursuits. Founded in 1977 by Annemarie Colbin.

AROMATHERAPY

BOOKS

Aromatherapy for Mother and Baby
Allison England
Healing Arts Press, 1993.
Natural healing with essential oils during pregnancy and early
motherhood.

Aromatherapy Kit
Charles E. Tuttle
Newsleaf,1993.
800 326-2665
112-page glossary of recommended oils along with a kit of five
essential oils known to have certain health benefits.

Holistic Aromatherapy
Christine Wildwood
Thorsens, 1986.
Instruction to promote health of body and serenity of mind with
essential oils.

Gattefosse's Aroamtherapy
Rene-Maurice Gattefosse
C.W. Daniel, 1937.
The first modern work written by the man who invented the word
'Aromatherapy'. Describes his lifetime of research into essential oils.

the natural
gourmet

institute for
food
and health

The Aromatherapy Book for Vibrant Health and Beauty
Roberta Wilson
Avery Publishing
A practical A to Z reference to Aromatherapy treatment for health, skin, and hair problems using essential oils.

RECORDINGS

Soothing Scents and Sounds
The Relaxation Company
Classical music tapes and bath oils in giftbox.

PERIODICALS

Beyond Scents Newsletter
3379 S. Robertson Blvd
Los Angeles, CA   90034
800 677-2368 or 310 838-6122
Oriented toward professionals, but available to general public.

Common Scents Newsletter
P.O. Box 3679
South Pasadena, CA   91031
818 457-1742
Oriented toward professionals, but available to general public.

Inside Aromatherapy Newsletter
P.O.Box 6723
San Rafael, CA   94903
415 479-9121
Oriented toward professionals, but available to general public.

International Federation of Aromatherapists
Royal Masonic Hospital
Ravens Ct Park
London England W6 OTN
081-864-8066
Magazine oriented toward professionals, but available to general public.

International Journal of Aromatherapy
P.O. Box 750428
Petaluma, CA   94975-0428
707 778-6762
A reference guide respected by professionals for those just beginning to learn about Aromatherapy and its benefits. Published 4 times/year.

Scentsitivity Newsletter
P.O. Box 17622
Boulder, CO   80308
303 258-3791
Oriented toward professionals, but available to general public.

The Alliance News Quarterly
P.O. Box 750428
Petaluma, CA   94975-0428
707 778-6762
Oriented toward professionals, but available to general public.

SOURCES FOR PRODUCT

Alba Botanica
P.O. Box 12085
Santa Rosa, CA   95406
800 347-5211 or 707 575-3111
Unscented skin and body care products.

Aroma Vera
5901 Rodeo Rd
Los Angeles, CA   90016
800 669-9514 or 310 280-0407
Essential oils and accessories.

Aromatic Concepts
12629 N Tatum Blvd Suite 611
Phoenix, AZ   85032
602 861-3696
Essential oils and accesories.

Beauty Kliniek
3268 Governor Drive
San Diego, CA   92122
619 457-0191
Consumer and professional education in Aromatherapy.

Hobe Labs
201 S. Mckemy Avenue
Chandler, AZ   85226
800 528-4482 or 602 257-1950
Essential oils and accesories.

Leydet Oils
4611 Awani Court
Fair Oaks, CA   95628
916 965-7546
Essential oils and accessories.

Magick Botanicals
3412 W Macarthur Suite J-L
Santa Ana, CA   92704
714 957-0674
Unscented skin, body and hair care products.

Natural Oils International
12350 Montague Street
Pacoima, CA   91331
818 897-0536
Essential oils and accessories.

Nature's Gate
9200 Mason Avenue
Chatsworth, CA   91311
818 882-2951 or 800 327-2012
Unscented body lotions.

Omega Nutrition
6505 Aldrich Road
Bellingham, WA   98226
800 661-3529 604 322-8862
Unrefined organic oils.

Original Swiss Aromatics
P.O. Box 6842
San Rafael, CA   94903
415 459-3998
Essential oils and accessories.

Orjene Natural Cosmetics
5-43 48th Avenue
Long Island City, NY   11101
800 886-7536 or 718 937-2666
Unscented skin, body and hair care products; unscented men's products.

Oshadhi
15 Monarch Bay Plaza Suite 346
Monarch Beach, CA   92629
800 933-1008 or 714 240-1104
Essential oils and accessories.

Prima Fleur Botanicals
1201 R Anderson Drive
San Rafael, CA   94901
415 455-0957
One Ounce Minimum.

Quintessence Aromatherapy
P.O. Box 4996
Boulder, CO   80306
303 258-3791
Consumer and professional education in Aromatherapy.

Santa Fe Fragrance
P.O. Box 282
Santa Fe, NM   87504
505 473-1717
Essential oils.

Shikai
P.O. Box 2866
Santa Rosa, CA   95405
800 448-0298 or 707 584-0298
Unscented body lotions.

Source Vital
3637 W Alabama Suite 146
Houston, TX   77027
800 880-6457
Essential oils, unscented skin and body care products, dead sea
salts, seaweed and algae products.

The Body Shop
45 Horsehill Road
Cedar Knolls, NJ   07927
800 541-2535
Retail outlets and direct to consumer catalogs offering a wide range
of personal care and aromatherapy products made exclusively from
natural ingredients.

Time Labs
P.O. Box 3243
South Pasadena, CA   91031
818 300-8096
Essential oils and accessories.

Windrose Aromatics
12629 N Tatum Blvd Ste 611
Phoenix, AZ   85032
602 861-3696
Essential oils and accessories.

ORGANIZATIONS

Aromatherapy Institute & Research
P.O. Box 2354
Fair Oaks, CA   95628
916 965-7546
Consumer and professional education in aromatherapy.

Aromatherapy Seminars
1830 S Roberston Blvd Suite 203
Los Angeles, CA   90035
800 677-2368 or 310 838-6122
Consumer and professional education in aromatherapy.

National Association for Holistic Aromatherapy
P.O. Box 1722
Boulder, CO   80308
303 258-3791
Aromatherapy professionals and educational programs.

Pacific Institute of Aromatherapy
P.O. Box 6723
San Rafael, CA   94903
415 479-9121
Consumer and professional education in aromatherapy.

The American Alliance of Aromatherapy
P.O. Box 750428
Petaluma, CA   94975-0428
707 778-6762
Aromatherapy professionals and educational programs.

The American Society for Phytotherapy & Aromatherapy
P.O. Box 3679
South Pasadena, CA   91031
818 457-1742
Aromatherapy professionals and educational programs.

The Preferred Source
3637 W. Alabama Suite 146
Houston, TX   77027
800 880-6457
Consumer and professional education in aromatherapy.

BREATH & VOICE

BOOKS

The Conscious Ear
Alfred A. Tomatis
Station Hill Press, 1991.
The fascinating autobiography of the French scientist and his
pioneering research into the ear-voice connection to health.

Dr. Breath
Carl & Reese Stough
William Morrow & Co., Inc. 1970; The Stough Inst., 1981.
An absorbing account of the most significant advancements of the
century in the knowledge of breathing.

Music and Miracles
Don Campbell
Quest Books, 1992.
Using music for transformational experiences. Described by 25
experts in the field of medicine, theology, psychology, and music.

Music: Physician for Times to Come
Don Campbell
Quest Books, 1990.
An anthology that covers music's healing abilities from shamanism
to guided imagery, from research in auditory stimulation to chant.
25 fine chapters.

*One Hundred Ways to Improve Your Teaching with Your
    Voice & Music*
Don Campbell
Zephyr, 1992.
Easy exercises for voice and for listening.

The Roar of Silence
Don Campbell
Quest, 1989.
The basic book on toning and self-generated healing sounds.

Healing Sounds - The Power of Harmonics
Jonathan Goldman
Element Inc, 1992.
An easy introduction to the healing aspects of sound.

The Healing Voice
Joy Gardener- Gordon
The Crossing Press, 1993.
An intuitive introduction to healing through vocal expression.

Case Studies in Music Therapy
Kenneth E. Bruscia, Ph.D.
Barcelona Publishers, 1991.
Fully documented references in every phase of music therapy.

Taoist Ways to Transform Stress into Vitality
Mantak Chia
Healing Tao Books, 1985.
An inside introduction into Chinese health techniques using the voice.

Diagnostic Use of the Infant Cry
P.F. Ostwald
Phibbs And Fox, 1968.
Early reference to the use of voice with infants and children.

Soundmaking
P. F. Ostwald
Charles Thomas Publishing, 1963.
Early reference to the use of voice with infants and children.

The Voice of Neurosis
Paul J. Moses
Grune And Stratton, 1954.
A basic medical sourcebook for sounds within the speaking and singing voice.

When Listening Comes Alive
Paul Madaule
Moulin Publishing, 1993.
A clear book about the importance of listening and the work of Dr. Alfred Tomatis.

The Singing Cure
Paul Newham
Shambalah, 1994.
Excellent text on using the voice as therapy.

The Tao of Voice
Stephen Chun-Tao Cheng
Destiny Books, 1991.
Combines the best of Western vocal techniques and modern psychophysical exercises with ancient Chinese philosophy and breathing practices to develop your vocal identity.

Sacred Sounds - Transformation Through Music and Word
Ted Andrews
Llewellyn Publications, 1992.
A simplified introduction to the metaphysical use of sounds.

RECORDINGS

Chant: The Healing Power of Voice and Ear
Don Campbell
Institute For Music, Health & Education
An intuitive introduction to healing through vocal expression.

Heal Yourself with Your Own Voice
Don Campbell
Institute For Music, Health & Education
Explainations and exercises of how to use your voice for healing.

Healing with Great Music
Don Campbell
Institute For Music, Health & Education
Descriptions of auditory and psychological improvement through better listening and classical music.

Healing with Tone and Chant
Don Campbell
Institute For Music, Health & Education
2 cassette tapes. Auditory exploration into the healing powers of the voice as well as the research of Dr. Alfred Tomatis.

ORGANIZATIONS

Institute for Music, Health & Education
P.O. Box 4179
Boulder, CO   80306
800 490-4968
A non-profit educational institute dedicated to the exploration of the sonic arts in education and therapy for innovative students and professionals. Offers workshops and certification programs focusing on the use of sound and music in wellness, personal growth and the exploration of human potential.

The Carl Stough Institute of Breathing Coordination
200 East 66 Street
New York, NY   10021-6728
212 308-7138
Continuing education program in respiratory science.

MUSIC FOR RELAXATION

BOOKS

Music and Sound in the Healing Arts
John Beaulieu
Station Hill, 1987.
Insights and learning about sound, music, noise, elemental archetypes, life energy, and healing.

Sounding the Inner Landscape: Music as Medicine
Kay Gardner
Caduceus Publications, 1990.
P.O. Box 27
Stonington, ME   04681
Offers insights into the origins and mysteries of music and sound as related to self-healing and healing others. Illustrated. "Sounding The Inner Landscape" cassette is a companion to book.

RECORDINGS

Ten Minutes to Relax Vol 1,2,3,4
The Relaxation Company
Spoken-word instructional relaxation tapes.

Nature Meditations
Andrew Stewart
The Relaxation Company
Windchimes, pan solo keyboard pieces combined with nature sounds and pipes, flutes, etc.

Soundscapes
Andrew Stewart
The Relaxation Company
Solo keyboard pieces combined with sounds of nature and windchimes, pan pipes and flutes, etc.

The Tao of Cello
David Darling
The Relaxation Company
CD or cassette. Collection of solo cello pieces.

Essence
Don Campbell
Institute For Music, Health & Education
A CD of fine music, new recordings of "Crystal Meditation" and the ballet suite "Dances For A Sleepwalker."

Healing Harmonies
Jim Oliver
The Relaxation Company
CD or cassette. Soothing music for relaxation.

Amazon
Kay Gardner
Ladyslipper, Inc.
800 634-6044
Flute meditations are blended with on-site natural recordings of the
Amazon River. CD or cassette.

Avalon
Kay Gardner
Ladyslipper, Inc.
Solo flute meditations that were recorded when Kay co-led a
women's mysteries tour in Glastonbury, England. Cassette.

Emerging
Kay Gardner
Ladyslipper, Inc.
An instrumental masterpiece by Kay and a host of other classical
muscians. Cassette.

Fishersdaughter
Kay Gardner
Ladyslipper, Inc.
A primarily vocal, traditional sound. All songs directly relate to
woman's power and story. Cassette.

Garden of Ecstasy
Kay Gardner
Ladyslipper, Inc.
A mixture of many cultures are blended in these musically healing
cassettes and tapes. Structured to take the listener through joy,
then resolution. CD or cassette.

Moods & Rituals
Kay Gardner
Ladyslipper, Inc.
A meditation of solo flutes to relax you into a state of tranquility.
Cassette.

Mooncircles
Kay Gardner
Ladyslipper, Inc.
Ancient flute compositions perfect for meditation or love-making.
Cassette.

Ocean Moon
Kay Gardner
Ladyslipper, Inc.
A collection of Kay Gardner's most important works. CD.

OneSpirit
Kay Gardner/Nurudafina Pill Abena
Ladyslipper, Inc.
A flute and percussion journey of global musics and rhythms spanning four continents. CD or cassette.

A Rainbow Path
Kay Gardner
Ladyslipper, Inc.
A relaxing, acoustic meditative instrumental performed by numerous instruments such as flute, harp, oboe, clarinet and cello.

Sounding the Inner Landscape
Kay Gardner
Ladyslipper, Inc
Guided meditation and music designed to accompany Kay Gardner's book of the same title.

Global Meditation
Various
Ellipsis Arts
4 CD/cassette set with booklet. Spiritual, ritual and meditative music from 40 countries and traditions.

Musical Massage Vol 1,2,3,4
Various Artists
The Relaxation Company
One hour CD/cassettes of soothing instrumental music to create a calming ambiance.

VIDEOS

Of Sound Mind and Body
Various
Macro Media
800 333-9185
An unforgettable voyage of discovery to the limits of our knowledge about sound, healing and the " vibrational structure" which underpins the cosmos.

SOURCES FOR PRODUCT

Ellipsis Arts
20 Lumber Road
Roslyn, NY   11576
800 788-6670
World music CD's and cassettes including boxed sets of traditional
music from around the world. Free catalog.

Ladyslipper, Inc.
P.O. Box 3124
Durham, NC   27715
800 634-6044 or 919 683-1570
Extensive catalog of women's music.

Original Music Catalog
418 Lasher Road
Tivoli, NY   12583
914 756-2767 or 914 756-2027
World Music CDs and cassettes from Africa, Asia, Black Diaspora,
Caribbean, Europe, Middle East.

The Relaxation Company
20 Lumber Road
Roslyn, NY   11576
800 788-6670
Tools for relaxation include CD's, cassettes, massage kits etc.
Free catalog.

World Music Institute
49 West 27 Street Suite 810
New York, NY   10001
212 545-7536 or 212 889-2771
A catalog of recordings, books and videos from all over the world.

ORGANIZATIONS

Glen Velez Drumming Workshops
P.O. Box 955
New York, NY   10024
212 595-5284
World renownded percussionist Velez shares the relaxation magic
of the ancient frame drum through workshops.

National Association for Music Therapy
1133 Fifteenth St NW
Washington, DC   20005
Holds conferences about music education for music therapists.

Olatunji Music
2109 Broadway Suite 477
New York, NY   10023
212 645-0388
Drummer Babantunde Olatunji teaches high-energy african drumming and dance workshops for both adults and children.

CREATIVE VISUALIZATION

BOOKS

Healing Visualizations
Gerald Epstein, M.D.
Bantam, 1989.
An exploration of guided imagery for healing with specific exercises.

Visualization for Change
Patrick Fanning
New Harbinger, 1988.
A complete guide to visualization including guided visualizations on many topics.

Awakening
Shakti Gawain
Nataraj Publishing, 1991.
A daily meditation guide that focuses on maintaining our spiritual center not just when we are in solitude, but when we are active in the world and in relationships.

Creative Visualization
Shakti Gawain
New World Library, 1978.
Easy to use techniques to feel more relaxed and peaceful, increase vitality and improve health, develop creative talents, etc.

Creative Visualization Workbook
Shakti Gawain
New World Library, 1982.
A companion volume to "Creative Visualization."
Provides convenient format to write down and practice many creative visualization techniques.

Living in the Light
Shakti Gawain & Laurel King
New World Library, 1986.
A practical guide for anyone who desires to develop their intuition and learn to follow it, using their creative abilities to the fullest.

Living in the Light Workbook
Shakti Gawain
Nataraj Publishing, 1991.
Includes 43 new exercises and meditations to help develop intuition, explore unconscious beliefs, and achieve better health.

Meditations
Shakti Gawain
New World Library, 1991.
Contains the meditations and visualization techniques from Shakti's audio cassette series, "Meditations With Shakti Gawain."

The Path of Transformation: How Healing Ourselves can
*   Change the World*
Shakti Gawain
Nataraj Publishing, 1993.
Confronts our global healing crisis and tells what each of us must do to save our planet.

Reflections in the Light: Daily Thoughts and Affirmations
Shakti Gawain
New World Library, 1988.
Designed to be read every day. 366 reflections selected from the author's classic works.

Return to the Garden
Shakti Gawain
Nataraj Publishing, 1989.
Describes the author's vision of the future: ancient wisom and modern technological intelligence combined.

VIDEOS

Creative Visualization Workshop Video
Shakti Gawain
New World Library
100-minute video workshop recorded live and packed with information and exercises.

The Path of Transformation: How Healing Ourselves can
*   Change the World*
Shakti Gawain
Nataraj Publishing
Confronts our global healing crisis and tells what each of us must do to save our planet.

RECORDINGS

Creative Visualization
Shakti Gawain
New World Library
Cassette. Powerful meditations and techniques taken from the book of the same title.

Living in the Light
Shakti Gawain
New World Library
An hour-long interview that reveals principles and techniques from the book of the same title. Cassette.

Developing Intuition
Shakti Gawain
New World Library
Cassette. Specific suggestions on how you can recognize the voice of intuition and allow it to become the guiding principle in your life.

Meditations with Shakti Gawain
Shakti Gawain
New World Library
A series of 4 audio cassettes: Contacting Your Inner Guide, The Male and Female Within, Discovering Your Inner Child, Expressing Your Creative Being.

The Path of Transformation: How Healing Ourselves can Change the World
Shakti Gawain
Nataraj Publishing
Cassette.Confronts our global healing crisis and tells what each of us must do to save our planet.

Relationships as Mirrors
Shakti Gawain
Focuses on what makes relationships work- not only intimate, but family and work relationships as well.

SOURCES FOR PRODUCT

Nataraj Publishing
P.O. Box 2627
Mill Valley, CA   94942
800 949-1091
Publishing company that provides books and tapes on the leading edge in the fields of personal and social consciousness growth.

New World Library
58 Paul Drive
San Rafael, CA   94903
415 472-2100 or 415 472-6131
A catalog of books and cassettes to improve the quality of life.
Titles include: "Expressing Your Creative Being," "The Perfect Life",
"Stop Improving Yourself And Start Living".

OHASHIATSU TOUCH

BOOKS

Do-It-Yourself Shiatsu
W. Ohashi
E P Dutton, 1976.
How to perform the ancient Japanese art of acupuncture without
needles on yourself and friends.

*Natural Childbirth the Eastern Way: A Healthy Pregnancy and
    Delivery Through Shiatsu*
W. Ohashi
Ballantine, 1983.
Available through The Ohashi Institute.

Reading the Body: Ohashi's Book of Oriental Diagnosis
W. Ohashi
Penguin/Arkana, 1991.
A guidebook to read the body and tell what Shiatsu techniques to
apply to the various energy meridians of the body. Illustrated.

Touch for Love: Shiatsu for Your Baby
W. Ohashi
Ballantine, 1984.
A step-by-step guide through the world of touch, showing you in
over 200 photographs how to tone your baby's skin and muscles,
stimulate growth, circulation, and mental awareness.

Zen Shiatsu
W. Ohashi And Masunaga
Japan Publications, 1977.
An unusual and valuable primer for people interested in
home remedies.

VIDEOS

Art of Ohashi Video Library
Ohashi International. Ltd, 1991.
Technique demonstration videos that teach a more advanced
approach to improve and create skillful body movement.

Ohashiatsu for a Healthy and Happy Pregnancy
Ohashi Institute, 1985.
212 684-4190
A step-by-step method of the Eastern way to achieve harmony between parents and child.

SOURCES FOR PRODUCT

Royal Pyramid, Inc.
414 Manhatten Avenue
Hawthorne, NY   10532
800 325-7423
A leading supplier of massage supplies and equipment. Free catalog and literature available upon request.

ORGANIZATIONS

American Association of Acupuncture
4101 Lake Boone Trail, Suite 201
Raleigh, NC   27607
610 433-2448
Available to consumers as a source for certified doctor referrals, education information and general information about acupuncture.

American Massage Therapy Association
820 Davis Street Suite 100
Evanston, IL   60201-4444
708 864-0123 or 708 864-1178
A practitioner organization that offers consumer referrals to licensed professionals, educational programs and information on massage therapy.

Esalen Institute
Big Sur, CA   93920
408 667-3000
Esalen bodywork is taught as a part of a 130 hour massage-practitioner program that is California state-approved.

Swedish Institute, Inc.
School Of Massage Therapy
226 West 26 Street 5th Floor
New York, NY   10001
212 924-5900
Massage curriculum that is registered by the New York State Department Of Education for professional purposes. Graduates meet the requirements to take the N.Y State licensing examination, as well as in several other states.

The Ohashi Institute
12 West 27 Street
New York, NY   10001
212 684-4190 or 212 447-5819
Curriculum includes Shiatsu, Oriental Medicine, Meditation,
Movement Exercises, Theatre, Dance, Martial Arts.

CONSCIOUS EXERCISE

BOOKS

The Complete Guide to Exercise Videos
Collage Video Specialties
5390 Main Street NE Dept 1
Minneapolis, MN   55421
800 433-6769
Hundreds of vidoes and audio cassettes divided into categories like:
stretch/yoga/relaxation, etc.

The Relaxed Body Book: A High-Energy Anti-Tension Program
T. Goleman, T. Bennitt-Goleman
Doubleday, 1986.
A program designed to relax the body due to everyday stress
and tension.

No Ordinary Moments
Dan Millman
H.J. Kramer, Inc.
A complete guide to the peaceful warrior's way and a powerful
impetus to personal growth.

Quest for the Crystal Castle
Dan Millman
H.J. Kramer, Inc.
800 400-0301
Children's book. A journey through a mysterious forest reveals
the power of kindness and each child's ability to overcome
life's obstacles.

Sacred Journey of the Peaceful Warrior
Dan Millman
H.J. Kramer, Inc.
The adventure continues as Dan meets a woman shaman in a
Hawaiian rainforest.

Secret of the Peaceful Warrior
Dan Millman
H.J. Kramer, Inc.
Children's book. Illustrated story of wisdom, magic and mystery.

The Inner Athlete
Dan Millman
Stillpoint, 1973.
A road-map to releasing your full potential as a "natural athlete" and reaching beyond goals to your dreams based on universal principles to enhance the quality of everyday life.

The Life You Were Born to Live
Dan Millman
H.J. Kramer, Inc.
A guide to finding your life purpose, and the spiritual laws to fulfill your destiny.

The Warrior Athlete: Body, Mind & Spirit
Dan Millman
H.J. Kramer, Inc.
Self-transformation through total training.

Way of the Peaceful Warrior
Dan Millman
H.J. Kramer, Inc.
The story that has touched a million lives. Also available on audio tape.

The Eight Pieces of Brocade
Dr. Yang Jwing-Ming
Yang Martial Arts Association
A Waidan Chi Kung exercise set for maintaining and improving health.

The Essence of Tai Chi Chi Kung
Dr. Yang Jwing-Ming
Yang Martial Arts Association
Ties Tai Chi and Chi Kung together.

The Root of Chineses Chi Yung
Dr. Yang Jwing-Ming
Yang Martial Arts Association
A bird's eye view of Chi Kung as related to martial arts, healing, spiritual training and intellectual development.

Yang Style Tai Chi Chuan
Dr. Yang Jwing-Ming
Yang Martial Arts Association
A fundamental book.

RECORDINGS

Life Purpose Audio Tape
Dan And Joy Millman
P.O. Box 6148
San Rafael, CA 94903
800 400-0301
Essential information about your life purpose related to health,
relationships, talents, work, and finances.

Energizing the Body
Dan Millman
800 400-0301
A 6-tape, 3-hour program with highlights in training body, mind,
and spirit; breath relaxation, and healing powers of the basic self.

Opening to Spirit
Dan Millman
800 400-0301
A 6-tape, 3-hour program with highlights in accepting emotions,
stairway to the soul, and making a difference.

The Five-Hour Audio Course
Dan Millman
Provides practical methods for mental clarity, physical vitality, and
inner peace in the midst of daily life.

The Path of Self-Discovery
Dan Millman
800 400-0301
A 6-tape, 3-hour program with highlights in clearing the mind,
balancing the psyche, and becoming your higher self.

The Power to Change
Dan Millman
800 400-0301
A 6-tape, 3-hour progam with highlights in overcoming addictions,
the will to change, and the right career.

The School of Life
Dan Millman
800 400-0301
A 6-tape, 3-hour program with highlights in money and spirit,
relationship and sexuality, and the laws of spirit.

The Peaceful Warrior Workout Video
Dan Millman
P.O. Box 6148
San Rafael, CA   94903
800 400-0301 or 415 491-0856
45-minute video that combines yoga, martial arts, gymnastics, dance, and fitness training.

SOURCES FOR PRODUCT

Peaceful Warrior Services
Dan Millman
Books, videos, recordings, lectures, seminars and trainings focusing on obtaining inner peace both psychologically and physically.

YMAA Product Catalog
38 Hyde Park Ave
Jamaica Plain, MA   02130
800 669-8892
Catalog offering books, videos, music, clothing and products on various subjects including Chi Kung, Tai Chi Chuan, and Hua Ching Ni.

NEW TECHNOLOGIES

BOOKS

Biocircuits: Amazing New Tools for Energy Health
Leslie And Terry Patten
H.J. Kramer, Inc. 1988
For home use. Biocircuits balance and magnify the body's natural energy, provide a strong and direct experience of life force, and serve as self-empowering tools for health, personal growth, and inner exploration.

A Short History of Light & Sound Technology
Michael Hutchison
Tools For Exploration
A guidebook to tips and insights into getting the most from light and sound.

Megabrain: New Tools And Techniques for Brain Growth
and Mind Expansion
Michael Hutchison
Ballantine, 1986, 1991.
A look at the recently developed machines and devices that may soon allow us to increase brain size and intelligence.

Megabrain Power
Michael Hutchison
Hyperion, 1994.
Latest scientific findings of new strategies, techniques and machines that enhance mental capabilities.

The Book of Floating: Exploring the Private Sea
Michael Hutchison
Morrow, 1984.
In-depth study of the effects and uses of flotation tanks.

Clinical Guide to Light and Sound
Thomas Budzynski
Tools For Exploration, 1991.
A clinical guide intended for psychotherapists and a significant contribution to the growing understanding of light/sound stimulation.

RECORDINGS

Megabrain Zones
Michael Hutchison
Megabrain Communications, Inc., 1993.
A 6-tape series that incorporates the latest in audio psycho-technology, environmental sounds and intuitive musical accompaniment to create some of the most advanced consciousness enhancement tools available.

PERIODICALS

Megabrain Report
Michael Hutchison
Megabrain Communications
In-depth and timely information on the cutting edge of technology and human consciousness. Published 4 times a year.

ORGANIZATIONS

The Biofeedback & Psychophysiology Clinic
The Menninger Clinic
P.O. Box 829
Topeka, KS   66601-0829
913 273-7500
Offers services for a wide variety of stress related and other health problems.

SOURCES FOR PRODUCT

Megabrain Communications
P.O. Box 2744
Sausalito, CA   94966
415 332-8323
The distributor of books and tapes by Michael Hutchison.
Subjects focus on cutting edge technologies on heigthening states
of consciousness and using sound to alter brainwave activity.

Tools for Exploration
Terry Patten
4460 Redwood Highway Suite 2
San Rafael, CA   94903
800 456-9887 or 415 499-9047
The most complete consumer catalog for cutting edge products and
resources on technologies that explore brain and mind potentials.
Categories include: biocircuits, biofeedback, electro-acupuncture,
new science and subtle energy products.

ALSO OF INTEREST:

PERIODICALS

The Newsletter of the American Institute of Stress
124 Park Avenue
Yonkers, NY   10703
800 24-RELAX
A monthly newsletter available to the public. Stress and health articles written by doctors.

ORGANIZATIONS

The American Institute of Stress
124 Park Avenue
Yonkers, NY 10703
800 24-RELAX
Dedicated to advancing our knowledge of mind-body relationships and the role of stress in health and illness.